Law, Governance and Technology Series

Volume 45

Series Editors

Pompeu Casanovas, Institute of Law and Technology UAB, Barcelona, Spain
Giovanni Sartor, University of Bologna and European University Institute of Florence, Florence, Italy

The *Law-Governance and Technology Series* is intended to attract manuscripts arising from an interdisciplinary approach in law, artificial intelligence and information technologies. The idea is to bridge the gap between research in IT law and IT-applications for lawyers developing a unifying techno-legal perspective. The series will welcome proposals that have a fairly specific focus on problems or projects that will lead to innovative research charting the course for new interdisciplinary developments in law, legal theory, and law and society research as well as in computer technologies, artificial intelligence and cognitive sciences. In broad strokes, manuscripts for this series may be mainly located in the fields of the Internet law (data protection, intellectual property, Internet rights, etc.), Computational models of the legal contents and legal reasoning, Legal Information Retrieval, Electronic Data Discovery, Collaborative Tools (e.g. Online Dispute Resolution platforms), Metadata and XML Technologies (for Semantic Web Services), Technologies in Courtrooms and Judicial Offices (E-Court), Technologies for Governments and Administrations (E-Government), Legal Multimedia, and Legal Electronic Institutions (Multi-Agent Systems and Artificial Societies).

More information about this series at http://www.springer.com/series/8808

Elisabeth Wilson-Evered • John Zeleznikow

Online Family Dispute Resolution

Evidence for Creating the Ideal People and Technology Interface

Springer

Elisabeth Wilson-Evered
Institute of Health and Sport
Victoria University
Melbourne, VIC, Australia

John Zeleznikow
Law School
La Trobe University
Melbourne, VIC, Australia

ISSN 2352-1902 ISSN 2352-1910 (electronic)
Law, Governance and Technology Series
ISBN 978-3-030-64644-8 ISBN 978-3-030-64645-5 (eBook)
https://doi.org/10.1007/978-3-030-64645-5

This Springer imprint is published by the registered company Springer Nature Switzerland AG.
The registered company address is: Gewerbestrasse 11, 6330 Cham, Switzerland

Foreword

This is a valuable book, written by two renowned scholars. The title is self-explanatory: *Online Family Dispute Resolution: Evidence for Creating the Ideal People and Technology Interface.* It is not just a work on resolving family disputes online but provides even evidence. Elisabeth Wilson-Evered is specialised in innovation and transformation within organisations. Her psychology background is perfectly complimentary with John Zeleznikow's expertise in dispute resolution and information systems. A dream team, to borrow terminology from the sports domain Elisabeth also works in: "In the sport context, her passion is on leadership integrity and creating system-wide leadership to address corruption and unethical behaviour". Before I deliver some comments on the content of the book, first some personal words against the background of my take on the field of ODR.

Over 25 years ago, in December 1993, I first met John Zeleznikow, when he presented at a conference in Florence. This was a memorable conference, and the environment, to me obviously in particular the river, Arno, is special. I did return only twice. In 2008 to deliver a keynote at the international ODR workshop, part of a successful series John and I started in 2003 in Edinburgh. That meeting was fruitful and attended by a little over 30, quite influential people: Ethan Katsh, Colin Rule, Ernie Thiessen, Orna Rabinovich, Julia Hörnle, Ben Davis, and many more.

A week ago I visited Florence for the third time, at the *Inaugural Conference of the IACL Research Group on Algorithmic State, Society and Market: Constitutional Dimensions.*[1] The times they are a changin'. In 2007, David Larson referred to this Bob Dylan song at his JURIX keynote on ODR, or technology-mediated disputed resolution as he calls it, and I also did believe in the opportunities of ODR back then. Right now, I am a bit cynical. During 2000–2008, the success of ODR seemed inevitable to me, from 2009 to 2013 I lost hope and interest, then I got optimistic

[1] http://www.algorithmicstate.eu/.

again because of the EU ADR Directive and ODR platform.[2] The recent evaluations (e.g. December 2017) of this platform, and the fact that hardly anyone has heard of it even three years after its launch, does not make me very hopeful.

Since the beginning days of ODR, low-value e-commerce disputes were seen as one of the most suited domains for the resolution of online disputes. First, because the dispute has an online origin, so it seems logical to resolve conflicts online after an online transaction. Second, because courts, in particular in an international context, are not fit for resolving these kind disputes and are also too expensive. The European Union is a big proponent of this argument. They adduced it 20 years ago, 10 years ago, and still today. Their argument is that consumers would trust cross-border e-commerce disputes better if they knew their conflicts would be adequately resolved. The European Union also believes that the amount of cross-border EU transactions is still low because of the lack of trust. However, for many years EU citizens buy from service providers in countries outside the EU. For 20 years they purchase from US websites, and over the last years from Chinese sites, notably Alibaba. Plus, consumers are not interested in resolving via ODR. Rather, they contact the seller directly or post a negative review. That is also what students at the London School of Economics said when I gave a guest lecture on ODR a couple of years ago. Last March, however, quite a few vLSE students in the same course believed that if ODR is convenient and inexpensive, consumers might be even interested in resolving low-value disputes by ODR. Clearly, the last word has not been spoken on this topic.

Where I no longer believe ODR is a right tool for low-value e-commerce disputes, I never lost faith in resolving family disputes online. I also regularly tell people about the interesting tools John Zeleznikow developed over the years. Like last week at the first meeting of the Dutch association for AI and Robot law, when I met an attorney specialised in criminal and family law, I told her about John and in particular his Family Winner (and to give it a popular twist, referred to his appearance with Emilia Bellucci in the national broadcasted New Investors TV show). The distribution mechanism of their program is appealing and easily explained so to award 100 points according to your preferences to the items in the estate. If you like the record albums, you give it 10 points, if not 1, etc. After this process, probably both ex-partners get over 70 out of 100 points they awarded to the items.

Back to the book. It contains six chapters. The first chapter sketches what happened over the last 20–30 years. The authors say "In Australia, mediation—generally facilitative mediation—has been used to handle disputes in the family arena for about twenty years", but since the footnote mentions the late 1980s we might as well say thirty years. From a legal perspective, an important development has been *The 2006 Reforms to the Australian Family Law Act.* I also learned a new term, OFDR: Online Family Dispute Resolution.

---

[2]Cortes, Pablo and Lodder, Arno R., Consumer Dispute Resolution Goes Online: Reflections on the Evolution of European Law for Out-of-Court Redress. *Maastricht Journal of European and Comparative Law* 2014/1, https://ssrn.com/abstract=2414098.

The second chapter is about Artificial Intelligence and ODR. It describes a wide range of very interesting programs. As is generally known: "For a long time, AI was confined to theory, but over the last 5 years in particular, due to progress in machine learning, AI is used by all big tech companies and many start-ups". [3] It is not necessarily machine learning that is used in OFDR, but the timing seems right to push these applications to a wider practical use.

The good news regarding my previous observation is witnessed in Chap. 3 on Current Research and Practice in Online Family Dispute Resolution that opens with "The exponential growth of Online Family Dispute Resolution (OFDR) means that consumers are now presented with a range of options on the market to suit their needs". And in addition, the evidence the authors provide stems positive: "Of those programs located by the review, it was evident that whilst more methodologically rigorous research is required, preliminary evidence shows support for OFDR effectiveness in reaching desirable and fair outcomes". Chapter 4 follows with an excellent and detailed case study on the Relationships Australia Queensland's Online Family Dispute Resolution System, and Chap. 5 includes cultural aspects related to indigenous people.

In the nicely elaborated Chap. 6, the authors share concluding thoughts. The authors state: "It has been the intention of this book to outline the current state of OFDR services as they are used within Australia. Although Australia has been identified as a leader in ODR and OFDR services, a comprehensive documentation of its history in the field, its services, and its unique considerations for service development and provision". I presume the authors meant to continue this sentence with something like "has wider meaning". I could not deny that. This book is an interesting account of one of the areas of dispute resolution where the use of online tools is a natural addition, if not (largely) replacement of offline practice.

Vrije Universiteit Amsterdam, Of Counsel SOLV Lawyers, Amsterdam, The Netherlands
19 May 2019

Arno R. Lodder

[3]A.R. Lodder (2019), Algorithms: what, how, and particularly why?, *LSE POLICY BRIEFING 34*, MAY 2019.

Preface

The Motivation for This Book

As inaugural Director of Research at Relationships Australia Queensland (RAQ), my research interests were piqued to the fascinating world of OFDR. Winning a project grant from the Federal Attorney General of Australia, Mark Thomson, then the Director of the Telephone Dispute Resolution Services (TDRS) sought to add behavioural science evidence and psychology to the project and included me. Professor Zeleznikow's internationally recognised expertise in technology applied to family law matters was also crucial.

Whilst we knew setting up technical infrastructure and application design might have challenges, disruptive and continuous innovations typically solve these issues rapidly. More enduring interest included what systems, human factors and human–computer interactions, acceptance and usefulness, and procedural factors in applying the law as well as ensuring confidentially would need critical attention when using OFDR with people who are potentially experiencing a traumatic event (divorce, separation, and child welfare issues). We sought to ask the clients and the mediators to consider how they might proceed through that process using an online platform rather than face-to-face. That work is represented in Chaps. 4 and 5 of this book.

What the Book Shares

The purpose of this book is to bring together in one volume the latest research evidence and practice on OFDR for the benefit of scholars, practitioners, policymakers, and government.

Chapter 1 discusses the evolution of Alternative Dispute Resolution within Australian Family Law. It discusses in detail, how the Family Law Act (1975) removed fault as a basis for decision-making and emphasised the paramount interests of children. The reforms of 2006, strongly encouraging the use of Family Dispute Resolution are examined. We then introduce how Online Dispute Resolution can be used to meet these goals.

Chapter 2 discusses how Artificial Intelligence can be used to support decision-making in Australian Family Law. Two early systems (Split-Up and Family Winner) are discussed in detail. Whilst these systems were initially designed for stand-alone personal computers, they are now available as online systems.

Chapter 3 presents a systematic and contemporary literature review of the scope the current research and practice evidence for Online Dispute Resolution in family law relating to child welfare. The use of OFDR services in both Australian and international contexts was investigated across a range of electronic sources since 2011. Of those programs located by the review, it was evident that whilst more methodologically rigorous research is required, preliminary evidence shows support for OFDR effectiveness in reaching desirable and fair outcomes.

Chapter 4 summarises processes, findings, and recommendations of a pilot OFDR implementation with Relationships Australia Queensland across the four stages of the program design: registration, intake, pre-FDR education, and OFDR. Clients and staff reported largely positive attitudes towards OFDR, with the need to appreciate the learning curve involved in navigating the system and how the technology qualitatively changes the mediation process.

Chapter 5 details an exercise in community engagement in planning for the roll out of services within Australia indigenous communities. Data included both focus groups and researcher reflections which were pooled and analysed leading to the development of key themes. Participating communities appear ready and enthused by the concept of online service delivery; however, they were wary of service provision that was not tailored to their needs or was culturally insensitive.

Concluding the book, Chap. 6 summarises the lessons learned to-date to inform recommendations for future OFDR program design and improvement. Both ODR and OFDR are relatively young developments in Australia and elsewhere, so the potential of these advanced technologies and their capabilities is yet unknown. Continued rigorous research into existing and future OFDR programs will further improve the field and the outcomes for families. Such an endeavour will take the collaboration of many different stakeholders and a commitment to ongoing learning and future-focused change.

Melbourne, VIC, Australia Elisabeth Wilson-Evered
Melbourne, VIC, Australia John Zeleznikow

Acknowledgements

Having conducted research in the domain of Law, Dispute Resolution, Information Technology and Law for almost thirty years, I naturally have many people to thank. My mentor, Don Berman, who sadly passed away twenty-five years ago, encouraged my passion for the domain. The colleagues and collaborators Dan Hunter, Arno Lodder, Noam Ebner, Uri Schild, Ruthie Kannai, Brooke Abrahams, Pompeu Casanovas, and Marta Poblet provided me with much useful support and advice. The PhD students and collaborators George Vossos, Andrew Stranieri, Emilia Bellucci, Peter Condliffe, Nadav Prawer, and Fahimeh Abedi helped develop ideas and/or software.

Without the dedication and support of my parents Masha and Abram Zeleznikow (who sadly both passed away in the past six years), I would never have started my research career forty-seven years ago. And of course, the wonderful support of our children Ashley, Sarah, Annie, Eva, and Joseph has encouraged me in my endeavours as well as providing me with much dispute resolution experience.

But the primary reason that I have been able to write this book, conduct research, raise children, and run marathons is because of the unlimited love and support of my wonderful life Lisa. Without her magnificent help, I could not have commenced writing the book, let alone completed the task.

John Zeleznikow

April 2019

This book, as all such endeavours, is the product of the work, support, encouragement, and help of others not the least my co-author Professor John Zeleznikow, an acknowledged world expert in the area of Online Family Dispute Resolution (OFDR). However, there have been many others and in particular those separating couples who contributed their experience to creating new understandings in this field.

Key people in the unique and innovative OFDR project discussed in Chaps. 4 and 5 were Mark Thomson, Stuart MacFarlane, Jennifer Murray, Tristan Casey, Natasha Rae, Samantha Klintworth, Shane Klintworth, Cindy McKenzie, Debra Bennet, Aunty Rose, amongst many others. Mark Thomas was especially important as his energy and focus and commitment to the success of the project surely led to its success. Professors John Zeleznikow and Pompeu Casanova were key instigators and encouraged drawing on the research evidence in the report to form the basis of the book. Though the report on OFDR began the journey and the proposal of this book, the current content was developed under John Zeleznikow's wisdom. I extend my sincere appreciation for his support. He in turn always relies upon the wonderful love of his wife Lisa.

Special acknowledgment and recognition are most deserved for Christina Maxwell's research and her work as a Production Assistant which led to the development of Chap. 3 and for the entire presentation and collation of this book. Her work has been invaluable and outstanding and the book would not have been completed without her skilful dedication to detail and evidence.

On a personal note, I thank my beloved mother for my drive and motivation to service and dedicate this book to her. She died in 2018 whilst I was writing this book. Other family members, colleagues, and friends have been wonderful supports throughout this period along with the unconditional love of my senior pets two dogs and cat which have sustained me. My sincere thanks to all.

Elisabeth Wilson-Evered

July 2019

P.S. With the advent of the COVID-19 pandemic in 2020, OFDR has moved from being a useful tool to an essential service!

Contents

Abbreviations

ABS	Australian Bureau of Statistics
ACMA	Australian Communications and Media Authority
ADR	Alternative Dispute Resolution
AIATSIS	Australian Institute of Aboriginal and Torres Strait Islander Studies
ASEAN	Association of Southeast Asian Nations
BATNA	Best Alternative to a Negotiated Agreement
CATI	Computer-assisted telephone interviewing
EU	European Union
FDR	Family Dispute Resolution
FDRP	Family Dispute Resolution Practitioner
FLA	Family Law Act
FRAL	Family Relationship Advice Line
FRC	Family Relationship Centre
ICT	Information and communication technologies
IT	Information technology
JA	Job analysis
LDS	List dispatching system
NHMRC	National Health and Medical Research Council
ODR	Online Dispute Resolution
OFDR	Online Family Dispute Resolution
PAR	Participatory action research
PDR	Primary Dispute Resolution
PPSS	Parent Plan Support System
RAQ	Relationships Australia Queensland
SAG	Secure Access Gateway
TDRS	Telephone Dispute Resolution Service

UNCITRAL	The United Nations Commission on International Trade Law
UTAUT	Unified theory of acceptance and use of technology
VoIP	Voice over Internet protocol
ZOPA	Zone of possible agreement

List of Figures

List of Tables

Chapter 1
The Evolution of Family Dispute Resolution and the Need for Online Family Dispute Resolution in Australia

Abstract Although dispute resolution has a long and rich documented history, the growth of out-of-court settlements and alternative dispute resolution (ADR) processes in Australia has been a recent development with family dispute resolution (FDR) services younger still. This chapter overviews the history of FDR in Australia to contextualise the development of online family dispute resolution (OFDR). As an extension to the already accessible Telephone Family Dispute Resolution service, OFDR offers the added value of multi-media engagement and innovative online tools to assist in easing the process of mediation for all stakeholders. From the introduction of the Family Law Act in Australia in 1975 to the 2006 Reforms, informal dispute processes are becoming recognised as fertile ground to deliver services via the use of advanced technologies. This chapter presents evidence as to the value of ADR in family law to mitigate issues concerning increased service demand, strained court resources, and the avoidance of emotionally taxing adversarial approaches. History shows a trend toward making services more efficient and effective, resulting in a natural progression to ODFR. Australia is currently at the forefront of OFDR advancement to accommodate their diverse and dispersed population.

1.1 Introduction

The general trend towards alternative forms of settling disputes has a substantial history and trajectory. The evolution of the ADR process and precursors; negotiation, arbitration and mediation, stem from pre-historic Shaman through the European Law Merchant to present times (Barrett and Barrett 2004).

Methods of dealing with disputes are enacted across nations today and these are often grounded in long standing social and religious belief systems of previous societies. Similarly, modes of dispute resolution we create in contemporary society will be expressed in various forms among future generations and societies. One major development in recent history is that of the World Wide Web and this particular innovation has changed how humans relate and do business and as a

E. Wilson-Evered, J. Zeleznikow, *Online Family Dispute Resolution*, Law, Governance and Technology Series 45,
https://doi.org/10.1007/978-3-030-64645-5_1

consequence also manage disputes. Taking just one platform for Alternative Dispute Resolution (ADR)—the family law context—this book proposes that not only is ADR valuable because of its traditional benefits such as: lower cost; greater speed; more flexibility in outcomes; less adversarial; more informal; solution rather than blame-oriented and privacy, but because it can involve large numbers, spread across many countries and in high demand, the diverse application will result in the rapid development of alternative methodologies to deliver ADR—specifically online.

This chapter begins with a brief history of the development of ADR and focuses specifically on the Australian manifestation of ADR in Family Law matters. There has been a focus on alternative dispute resolution in the Family Court of Australia from its inception in 1975. Initially, conciliation and counseling were employed. It was not until the late 1980s that mediation began to be used.

After establishing the credentials for ADR, we move to discuss different ways of delivery and specifically, explore telephone and online methodologies for dispute resolution focusing particularly on family conflicts. Next, we consider a case study of telephone family dispute resolution and our main focus of online family dispute resolution. We share our learning from a pilot of establishing an online family dispute resolution service, which substantiates its promise. Finally, we present evidence to suggest the likely increase in demands for online approaches to ADR given the widely dispersed parties in disputes together with an increasing uptake and preference for online services for a sizable proportion of the client population now and into the foreseeable future.

1.2 Historical Development of Alternative Dispute Resolution

The substantial history of ADR has been documented by many scholars. Among them, Lodder and Zeleznikow (2010) argued that the resolution of disputes is one of the earliest forms of human endeavour. Citing examples from Moses who supposedly descended from Mount Sinai with the Ten Commandments and the six hundred and thirteen laws that can be found in the Torah, the authors present evidence of codification of ADR in ancient societies. These instructions, not only provided a context and laws for how Jews live their life, they also gave guidance on the way in which disputes could be resolved. Nonetheless, dispute resolution practices predated Jewish and later Christian societies.

The long tradition of litigation is characterised by formal and legal safeguards that ensure Judges are impartial and independent, and procedural fairness is part of the espoused guarantee. Of particular importance is the assurance of confidentiality particularly for businesses and where cases with public profile can have adverse implications for persons or corporate entities involved in a dispute.

An arguable turning point in the development of modern alternatives to litigation was when *National Conference on the Causes of Popular Dissatisfaction with the*

Administration of Justice, held in April 1976, took place. The USA Chief Justice at the time, Warren Burger, encouraged the exploration and use of informal dispute resolution processes. At that time, Sander (1976) introduced the idea of the Multidoor Courthouse.[1] Since 1976, Alternative Dispute Resolution has become the preferred form of dispute resolution in most common law jurisdictions. Galanter (2004) claimed:

> In the federal courts, the percentage of civil cases reaching trial has fallen from 11% in 1962 to 1.8% in 2002. In spite of a five-fold increase in case terminations, the absolute number of civil trials was 20% lower in 2002 than it was 40 years earlier.

In writing about the Vanishing American Trial, Galanter argued that whereas litigation in the United States had increased, the number of trials decided by US judges had declined drastically. Two of the reasons for this phenomenon were noted as being related to the average trial's duration becoming longer and more complex and litigants were adopting alternative forms of Dispute Resolution.

Most negotiations in law are conceivably conducted in the shadow of the Law so that bargaining in legal domains mimics the probable outcome of litigation. Mnookin and Kornhauser (1979) introduced the bargaining in the shadow of the trial concept. By examining the case of divorce law, they contended that the legal rights of each party could be understood as bargaining chips that can affect settlement outcomes. Similarly, Bibas (2004) noted that some scholars treated plea-bargaining as simply another case of bargaining in the shadow of a trial. Indeed, according to Cooter et al. (1982) Bargaining in the Shadow of the Law for civil cases dominates the literature on civil settlements.

1.2.1 *Global Adoption of ADR in Family Law*

Though the trend away from having decisions made by judges is increasingly the norm in civil and criminal law, it is especially so in Family Law. This section will provide a brief overview of the historical socio-cultural and legal developments toward mediation in family law across the globe.

U.S.A. The United States boasts one of the earliest formal services for family dispute resolution (FDR). California established the first 'court-connected conciliation service' for marriage disputes in 1939 and the Los Angeles Court offered a form of pre-mediation divorce counselling in 1995, however widespread acceptance and awareness of family mediation did not occur until the 1970s (Brown 1982; Milne et al. 2004). Of note was the development of the Family Mediation Centre in Atlanta,

[1]According to the United States Department of Justice, the term multi-door courthouse describes courts that offer an array of dispute resolution options or screen cases and then channel them to particular alternative dispute resolution processes. See www.usdoj.gov/adr/manual/Part3_Chap1.pdf last accessed June 24 2008.

Georgia in 1974 by O.J. Coogler. As the first private family mediation centre in the U.S., it signaled a growing awareness of the importance of offering alternative dispute resolution solutions that were non-adversarial (Milne et al. 2004). For a comprehensive overview of the historical developments of family mediation services in the U.S., the reader is directed to Brown (1982). Despite having a formidable lead in the development and implementation of FDR, there have been critiques about the lack of consistency between the states for mediator standards and family laws, which has implications for the practice of cross-border mediation (González Martín 2015).

British Columbia Canada also saw a rise in family mediation in the 1970s and 1980s, with 1984 being a particularly influential year (Boyle 2013). Both the Mediation Development Association of British Columbia and Family Mediation Canada were established, and the Law Society of British Columbia developed a set of conduct and practice rules for family mediators. The Family Justice Services Division was created in 1996 and came to offer mandated pre-education sessions ('parenting after separation') for disputing families before they entered the family court system. More recently, a new Family Law Act was enacted in 2013 to further support ADR for family dispute resolution, with a specific emphasis on ensuring the 'best interests of the child'.

Europe In 1998, the Council of Europe adopted *Recommendation No R (98)1 of the Committee of Ministers of the Council of Europe on Family Mediation* (Pali and Voet 2013). This recommendation promotes the preferential use of family mediation, guiding principles for practice, and the regulation of mediation, particularly in the area of divorce matters and custody cases of children. Further mediation principles were elucidated in 2004 through the *European Code of Conduct for All Mediators*, which included family disputes. European countries are not homogenous and therefore differ in their responses to family disputes and their application of family mediation, although it is recognized that all countries have adopted some ADR (Pawlowski 2007). For a discussion on the specific differences in FDR history between European countries, the reader is referred to Pawlowski (2007) and Casals (2005).

Hong Kong ADR was introduced in 1985 with the Hong Kong International Arbitration Centre (Sullivan 2005). Despite concerns about integrating mediation into the cultural climate of Hong Kong where divorce carries social stigma and shame, ADR has been viewed positively by the public in managing family disputes. In fact, ADR has been considered as being consistent with cultural beliefs and values, as mediation is child-focused and family oriented, and facilitates agreement with dignity and cooperation.

The Hague Convention The Hague Convention on the Civil Aspects of International Child Abduction (1980) aims to return children involved in cross-border parental abduction (González Martín 2015). It relies on the collaboration between contracting states, of which there are currently 85.[2] The Hague Convention demonstrates a child-focused perspective by emphasizing the prompt resolution of the issue in order to reduce distress and disorder in the child's life. Mediation is also endorsed as a useful tool in aiding the peaceful return of the child, which has been outlined both in the Guide to Good Practice on Mediation and the 1996 Hague Child Protection convention (Pali and Voet 2013). However, there are differences in uptake and adherence between contracting states (Zdenek 2014).

1.3 Appropriate Dispute Resolution in Australian Family Law

From the perspective of Australian history, the origins of ADR can be traced back thousands of years ago to the Aboriginal and Torres Strait Islander communities who engaged in dispute resolution practices among themselves (Spencer and Hardy 2014). After European invasion, the *Commonwealth Constitution* in 1901 lay the groundwork for dispute resolution, which was later documented more thoroughly in the *Commonwealth Conciliation and Arbitration Act 1904* (Cth). With this Act came the establishment of a Commonwealth Court to resolve workplace disputes.[3]

ADR did not begin to gain traction in Australia until the 1970s when the courts began to be perceived as restricting access to justice. As such, ADR was proposed as an alternative pathway to restoring justice for disputants (French 2007; Akin Ojelabi 2010). Further developments in the growth of ADR occurred in 1980 when Community Justice Centres were established in New South Wales to deliver dispute resolution services (French 2007; Spencer and Hardy 2014). These Centres are now retrospectively viewed as early adopters of ADR techniques.

It was around this time that an interest in ADR for family disputes began to flourish. McIntosh et al. (2009) have noted the adverse social, educational, and mental health effects of divorce on children. However, they have also identified various protective factors such as low parental conflict and amiable co-parenting. Therefore, it is crucial that separating families have access to a dispute process that minimises distress for all involved. Where court-led approaches were adversarial and emotionally taxing for separating families, ADR was considered as an effective and efficient alternative that has the ability to reduce hostility between disputing parties.

The concept of secular, fault-based divorce (introduced in England in 1857 by the *Matrimonial Causes Act 1857* (UK) 20 & 21 Vict, c 85) found their its way into the laws of the Colonies and then those of the Australian States. The *Matrimonial Causes Act 1959* (Cth) provided a list of 14 predominantly fault-based grounds on which divorce might be granted. In 1975, the Whitlam government introduced a new

[2]https://www.hcch.net/en/states/hcch-members last accessed 20 May 2020.

[3]See Spencer and Hardy (2014), p. 5 for a comprehensive timeline of developments in Australian ADR.

Family Law Act (FLA). The legislation, which came into effect in January 1976, introduced no-fault divorce and espoused a holistic approach to dispute resolution, with the setting up of a specialist family court complete with court-attached conciliation and counselling (Nicholson and Harrison 2000). The best-known feature of the Act was the introduction of no-fault divorce. The approach allowed for a divorce to be granted independently of the institution of proceedings and recognised that both parents have rights and responsibilities over their children after separation, unless a court orders otherwise. This requirement for both parents to care for their children led to the need for parents to continue having a relationship following their divorce.

The Family Law Act (1975) provided that a marriage may be dissolved on the application of one party who is able to prove that the parties have been separated for at least 12 months, the marriage being considered to have broken down irretrievably. No remedies are available for 'good' or 'bad' behaviour.[4]

Section 60CA of the *Family Law Act 1975* (Cth) states that, "in deciding whether to make a particular parenting order in relation to a child, a court must regard the best interests of the child as the paramount consideration." As Crowe and Toohey (2009) say "In practical terms, the paramountcy principle aspires to discourage an excessively adversarial approach to parenting agreements, thereby alleviating some of the harm that children suffer as a result of parental conflict."[5] Bagshaw (1999) says "The Family Law Reform Act 1995 (enacted on June 11, 1996) makes counselling, conciliation, and mediation the preferred methods of dispute resolution in family law in Australia (in particular where there are disputes over children), shifting the focus away from court-imposed solutions. The term primary dispute resolution (PDR) is used in preference to alternative dispute resolution (ADR) to convey the message that these methods are to be the principal dispute-resolution methods in family law matters."[6]

In sum, in Australia, mediation—generally facilitative mediation—has been used to handle disputes in the family arena for about twenty years.[7] The 'family arena' generally comprises property or child-related disputes arising between parents, whether married or not, and whether the parties have lived together or not. Such disputes may also involve other people, related to the children or who have cared for the children; however, the overwhelming majority of disputes mediated are couple-related.

The typical approach to mediation expected the couple enter mediation voluntarily. However, this is not the situation in Australia today: at least one meeting with a specialist family dispute resolution practitioner is mandatory before lodging an

[4]Much of these two paragraphs are taken from Nicholson and Harrison (2000), p. 763 and p. 764.

[5]At p. 392.

[6]At p. 390.

[7]Although there was a focus on alternative dispute resolution in the Family Court of Australia from its inception in 1975, conciliation and counseling were initially employed and it was not until the late 1980s that mediation began to be used.

application for a parenting order in the Family Court of Australia. The reasons for the change are complex. Certainly, a major factor in the past two decades has been the marked increase in the breakdown of family relationships, resulting in excessive workloads for courts dealing with family matters. Arguably, economic drivers have also played a significant role for at least two reasons. First, because of the limitations in the number of available judges and funding to the courts; and, second, because of the cost to the public purse of court action for matters which can be dealt with more expeditiously and cheaply by other means. Also influential is evidence that points to a major emotional cost to the family of court action; a situation seemingly incompatible with the 'best interests of the child' principle which theoretically governs family court actions. Finally, the success of voluntary dispute resolution has convinced decision-makers that mediation is a superior alternative to adjudication for the majority of family conflicts, whether undertaken voluntarily or not. As such, ADR is not only appropriate for family disputes, but it is also well suited to the Australian context in which a culture of ADR has clearly developed over the last few decades.

1.4 The 2006 Reforms to the Australian Family Law Act

In 2006, the Commonwealth government passed legislation (effective 1 July 2008) to make mediation a mandatory prerequisite for anyone seeking a parenting order with the usual exceptions for people in violent relationships or other situations involving gross power imbalances. Though the primary focus of family dispute resolution is to reach agreement, the method by which such agreements are reached can vary. For example, following assessment, the preferred approach may be one of mediation, conciliation, or judicial decision making. Notably, unlike industrial disputes, family disputes rarely use arbitration, though clearly such an approach is feasible. The increasing numbers of marital breakdowns, dispersion of families and technological innovations has transformed dispute resolution services to families. For example, though face to face remains an important mechanism for providing services, newer approaches including telephone dispute resolution and, online dispute resolution or a mix of each of these methods are proving invaluable. As a major step in the Family Law Reforms of 2006, the Australian government provided financial support to open a series of 65 family relationship centres. The centres were funded to provide information, advice, and dispute resolution to help people reach agreement on parenting arrangements without the need to go court. Parkinson (2013) claimed:

> Family Relationship Centres formed the centrepiece of major reforms to the family law system in Australia which were introduced from 2006 onwards. They provide information and advice and offer free or heavily subsidised mediation of parenting disputes. They are an early intervention strategy to help parents manage the transition from parenting together to parenting apart in the aftermath of separation, and are intended to lead to significant cultural change in the resolution of post-separation parenting disputes. While Family Relationship

> Centres have many roles, a key purpose is as an early intervention initiative to help parents work out post-separation parenting arrangements and manage the transition from parenting together to parenting apart. (p. 195)

The term mandatory mediation has often been used to describe the resolution of disputes regarding the care of children in Australia, However, the Family Law Act 1975 (Cth) uses the term Family Dispute Resolution which is defined as "...a process (other than a judicial process): a. in which family dispute resolution practitioners helps people affected, or likely to be affected, by separation or divorce to resolve some or all of their disputes with each other; and b. in which the practitioner is independent of all of the parties involved in the process".[8] Parties who are seeking any court orders in relation to parenting are required to make a 'genuine effort' to resolve their disputes through Family Dispute Resolution prior to initiating court proceedings.[9]

Brown and Marriott (1999) define mediation as

> A facilitative process in which disputing parties engage the assistance of an impartial third party, the mediator, who helps them to try to arrive at an agreed resolution of their dispute. The mediator has no authority to make any decisions that are binding on them, but uses certain techniques and skills to help them to negotiate an agreed resolution of their dispute without adjudication.

The essence of Australian Family Dispute Resolution is that whilst the practitioner is impartial between the parties, she does have a very specific role—to safeguard the paramount interests of the child.[10] In this capacity she is compelled, where necessary to offer advice about the care of children. A family dispute resolution practitioner (FDRP) will not encourage clearly unsuitable parenting plans—for example, she would advise against any plan that involves having the children move house on a daily basis.

For a matter regarding children's interests to be raised in the Family Court of Australia, a party must attempt Family Dispute Resolution, if the parties are unable to reach an agreement during Family Dispute Resolution or have a practitioner decide that the case is not suitable for family dispute resolution, after assessing both parties. There are exceptions when there are long-term domestic violence issues, or mental health or positional issues.[11]

Hence the process in Australia is described as Family Dispute Resolution rather than mediation. Given the very distinct differences between International Conflict Resolution and Family Dispute Resolution, we wonder if it is it even worthwhile considering the notions of readiness and ripeness to mediate in Family Dispute Resolution.

---

[8]Family Law Act 1975 (Cth) s 10F.

[9]Family Law Act 1975 (Cth) s 60I.

[10]Family Law Act 1975 (Cth) s 60CA.

[11]Family Law Act 1975 (Cth) s 60CF and 60CG.

1.5 Delivery Options for Family Alternative Dispute Resolution

Australian family dispute resolution has undergone rapid transformation in the space of 20 years. Beginning in the 1980s, mediation was considered an alternative form of dispute resolution. Over the next 15 years, mediation became a primary approach to dispute resolution which has culminated to the current times as a compulsory first step by 2008, if parents cannot reach agreement on arrangements for their children. The transition has been rapid when compared with the gradual changes that typically characterize the common law. Mediation has proven an effective way of dealing with family relationships reducing time and cost from a pragmatic perspective. Importantly, a substantial body of research demonstrates the detrimental effects of conflict between parents on their children. Together, these outcomes of parental conflict provide logical justification for Government policy. The determination for compulsory dispute resolution before parents are permitted to lodge an application for a parenting agreement in the courts is established practice Australia.

A recent report by Armstrong (2010) stated that in 2008–09 almost 23,000 clients in government funded Family Relationship Centres (FRCs) were provided with family mediation. Non-FRC community based services offered mediation or FDR to about 7000 clients.

In a major addition to traditional family dispute resolution services, the Australian Family Relationships Advice Line (FRAL)[12] provides the organisation of telephone dispute resolution for people assessed as more appropriate for the telephone medium than for face-to-face services. The Telephone Dispute Resolution Service (TDRS) was established through funding from the Federal Attorney General of the Australian Government in 2007 (Thomson 2009) and is based in Queensland, operated by Relationships Australia Queensland (RAQ) and has a service partnership with Relationships Australia (NSW). Potential clients cannot directly contact or self-refer to the TDRS; rather they need to be referred either through the Family Relationship Advice Line, a Family Relationships Centre, or any other government-funded Family Dispute Resolution provider.

On referral from FRAL or a FRC, clients discuss their requirements with TDRS staff and if appropriate register their dispute. Then, demographic details are recorded and advice given on the TDRS process and an intake appointment is scheduled. Such an approach arguably expedites the transition from first contact to agreement compared with the typical dispute resolution process at a FRC. Indeed, Fletcher (2008) quotes an average time of 94 days for men and 109 days for women from the time of initial interview to dispute resolution.[13]

[12]See http://www.familyrelationships.gov.au/Services/FRAL/Pages/default.aspx last accessed 30 August 2017.

[13]The time is longer for women as they are more likely to initiate the process and hence be the first party to be interviewed.

As Wilson-Evered et al. (2011) note, the service has experienced rapid growth with numbers increasing from 971 new registrations in the 2007/8 period to 3969 registrations in the 2008/9 period. In approximately 5% of cases at least one party identified as Indigenous and over 80% of calls are answered within 20 seconds (Thomson 2009).

Scheduling of the dispute resolution session is contingent on an assessment of the case by a senior practitioner. A series of screening and assessment questions are asked in line with the legal requirement for determining cases suitable for dispute resolution (Thomson 2009). As a percentage of family disputes involve domestic or family violence, the telephone approach is more feasible as couples disperse to avoid contact. Indeed, approximately 12% of cases involved issues relating to family violence or child abuse. Of note, given the increase in child abductions, the TDRS has seen a growth in referrals from the International Social Services including applications made under the Hague Convention on Civil Aspects of International Child Abduction.

Of the 2392 cases that were closed between 2008 and 2009, in 626—that is 26% of the cases—FDR was conducted. Of this number, full agreement was reached in terms of parenting agreements in 285 cases (45%), part agreement was reached in 193 cases (31%) and no agreement occurred in 148 cases (24%). In general, reporting suggests agreement is made between 75% and 85% of those cases referred to TRDS in the years since inception. The lower number represents current figures and is associated with the marked increase in cases being managed (Thomson 2009). In a report prepared for the Australian Family Court, the percentage of cases resolved through mediated agreements was 61% in 2004–5 and 60% in 2005–06.[14]

On average, 400 cases per month are referred to the TDRS indicating on the one hand, an increased demand for mediation that is not conducted in a face to face setting or, on the other, the dispersion of families across Australian and beyond, making face to face too expensive or impractical. The majority of family mediation or dispute resolution cases conducted since 2006 has occurred in FRCs (66%), the rest was provided by Legal Aid, lawyers and courts (10%), private counselling or mediation services (12%) and over the phone (2%) (Kaspiew et al. 2012).

[14] A discussion of the Australian Telephone Dispute Resolution System and the Online Family Dispute Resolution System can be found in Thomson (2011).

1.6 A Brief Introduction to the Potential of an Australian Online Family Dispute Resolution System

Online Dispute Resolution (ODR)[15] is the use of technology to assist in dispute resolution. Unlike the case in traditional offline processes, ODR by its nature needs Information Technology (IT) to resolve the conflict: in the online environment communication is inherently electronic. So, the role of technology is pivotal, and the involvement of IT is essential. This observation led Katsh and Rifkin (2001)[16] to introduce the notion of the fourth party. The identified that the following stakeholders can be identified in online dispute resolution:

- The two parties having the dispute;
- The independent third party (mediator, arbitrator, conciliator), and;
- The technology, referred to as a fourth party.

ODR is a concept developed circa 1996. At that time the focus was upon the resolution of disputes that originated online. The prevailing belief was that those disputes that originated on the internet would easily be resolved via the World Wide Web. For most of the past twenty years, ODR research has focused upon electronic commerce disputes. Only recently, has ODR focussed upon non-financial disputes and disputes that do not originate online.

A burgeoning interest in diversifying the use of ODR began with the 15TH ODR Conference, held in the Hague, Netherlands, 23–24 May 2016. It had as its focus *Can ODR really help courts and enhance access to justice.*[17] Issues that were considered included:

1. The collection of information online;
2. The provision of online advice; and
3. The ability to request judicial intervention online, e.g. obtaining domestic violence intervention orders online.

Indeed, the prospective program for the 2020 International ODR Forum[18] further built on this momentum by including themes such as:

1. The use of ODR in society, with an interest in family disputes;
2. Considerations of data privacy and data protection;
3. Sharing learnings and latest developments of ODR technology and the future of justice in ODR.

After two decades, the legal community is finally realising the potential for ODR to enhance Access to Justice. Chicago Kent College of Law teaches an *Access to*

---

[15]Also known as Technology Assisted Dispute Resolution, Technology Facilitated Dispute Resolution and Technology Based Dispute Resolution—see Wahab et al. (2012), p. 3.

[16]At pp. 93–94.

[17]See https://2016odr.wordpress.com/ last accessed September 13 2016.

[18]Intended to be held in Dublin, Ireland on May 6–7, ODR 2020 was postponed due to coronavirus (COVID-19) pandemic. See https://odr2020.org/ last accessed 11 May 2020.

Justice and Technology subject in its JD program.[19] Issues of ethics and governance are finally being considered (Ebner and Zeleznikow 2016) indicating that the field has become mature. Casanovas and Zeleznikow (2014) discuss how relational law, relational justice and regulatory systems be linked to the newer versions of ODR. Whilst there is a recently found interest in this topic amongst the legal community, academic discussions and research in this discipline first occurred at the birth of the internet—two decades ago—such as the third Annual Forum on Online Dispute Resolution held at the University of Melbourne Law School in 2004.

With the ready availability of personal computers and the development of the internet,[20] inevitably Information Communication Technologies (ICT) have a role to play. Such technologies can be used to enhance negotiation decision-making in a number of ways. For example, first, information technology can be used to build decision support systems as in Family Winner or Asset Divider (to be discussed further in Chap. 2; Lodder and Zeleznikow 2010) to help decision makers or litigants to make better decisions. Second, computer systems, programs and the internet can be used to deliver legal or associated services to assist people in disputes who may not be able or chose not to 'meet' face to face for a host of pragmatic and emotional reasons.

The uptake of ODR by Australian governments and organisations was initially slow. In Conley Tyler and Bretherton's review of existing ODR services in 2003, only 3.8% were identified as originating in Australia. NADRAC (2001) posited that the dominance of North American online ADR over Australia was the result of poor broadband infrastructure. The first Australian online ADR appeared in 2002 with the Department of Justice Victoria recognizing the potential of online-enhanced ADR for their services (Conley Tyler and Bretherton 2003). During this time, Conley Tyler and Bretherton suggested that Australia was in the 'institutional' phase of online ADR development, whereby governments and other formal institutions were beginning to recognise the advantages of integrating ODR into their services.

These days, Australia is leading the world in offering online methodologies for delivering dispute resolution services. In 2018, Victoria University in Melbourne hosted the ODR Conference (Online Dispute Resolution: The State of the Art Symposium) which provided a platform to showcase Australian initiatives in ODR.[21] Given Australia's vast continent, communications through technologies to deliver education, health care, scientific innovations and communication among

[19]See http://www.kentlaw.iit.edu/courses/jd-courses/jd-seminars/access-to-justice-and-technology last accessed November 20 2016.

[20]See for example the roll-out of the Australian Government's National Broadband Network theconversation.com/the-nbn-how-a-national-infrastructure-dream-fell-short-77780 last accessed 30 August 2017.

[21]https://www.odrmelbourne.com.au/ last accessed 19 May 2020.

parties have advanced at pace since the early times of 'the school of the air'.[22] Notably, geographical factors were a driving force for online ADR uptake, with few rural and remote physical services available and considerable costs incurred in the accessing of services by these communities (Sourdin and Liyanage 2012). Naturally, the dispersed population and the ever-increasing rate of divorce along with the need for containing costs has induced innovations in the conflict resolution space for both civilian and business customers.

The conditions for ODR success in Australia have also been assisted by an increased spread of internet and technology access across the country in both private and public environments over the last two decades (Sourdin and Liyanage 2012). Recent Australian Bureau of Statistics data show that 86% of Australian households in 2017 have access to the internet and that, of these households, 91% have access to computers and 91% have access to mobile phone devices.[23] As such, the current generation have grown up with online environments and are comfortable and proficient in their use (NADRAC 2001). Sourdin and Liyanage (2012) posit that the dual effects of these technology advancements and family law changes make Australia ripe for OFDR.

As aforementioned, the *Family Law Act 1975* (Cth) and the later 2006 Reforms have paved the way for family ADR, which in turn, laid the foundations for the TDRS. The success of the TDRS in Australia has demonstrated a public demand for alternative delivery modes of family dispute resolution services. It seems clear that a natural progression would be to investigate how family dispute resolution services could be enhanced by the capabilities of technology (Wilson-Evered et al. 2011). Indeed, as early as 2003 it was documented that the public were interested in accessing ODR (Conley Tyler and Bretherton 2003). In fact, the majority, if not all, dispute resolution service providers already utilize a form of technology in their practice (e.g., emailing clients, document sharing; Conley Tyler and McPherson 2006). Regarding readiness for OFDR, it appears that Australia as a nation has the technological capacity to support the development and implementation of such services, FDRPs have indicated readiness to adapt their practices (Casey and Wilson-Evered 2012), and potential consumers are ready (Conley Tyler and Bretherton 2003).

As Zeleznikow (2014) notes, family mediation can be well supported through the use of online tools, because

1. We can learn from many prior disputes,
2. They are generally micro in nature (compared to international disputes) and the disputants in conflict do not use agents.

To have a viable, comprehensive Online Family Dispute resolution we believe the following issues need to be more closely re-searched.

---

[22]See School of the Air http://www.australia.gov.au/about-australia/australian-story/school-of-the-air last accessed August 30 2017.

[23]See https://www.abs.gov.au/ausstats/abs@.nsf/mf/8146.0 last accessed 19 May 2020.

1. Pre Family Dispute Resolution Education

    - It is important to educate or make clear to parents about the impact of parental separation and dysfunctional parental conflict on the child/children
    - It is important to promote positive cooperative co-parenting styles
    - It is important to prepare parents for the mediation process—practically, emotionally, and cognitively
    - It is important to direct parents to other resources, such as counselling and/or other parenting programs.

Pre Family Dispute Resolution education might include the provision of legal education such as appropriate legislation and cases; and the provision of workbooks, and videos to encourage appropriate behaviour during the dispute resolution process. This information will be made available to face-to-face and TDRS clients as well as OFDR users.

Our belief is that the provision of such services will diminish unreasonable behaviour, leading to less belligerent disputes, parents focusing more upon the interests of their children rather than their own desires and a quicker resolution of disputes.

2. Provision of Advice About Negotiation Strategies

Bellucci and Zeleznikow (2006) used the principles of cooperative game theory developed by Nash (1953) into their Family Winner system. The Family Winner software develops a strategy to decide which of the parties in a divorce gains particular items that have been valued by each party. The program uses game theory and a system of underlying rules (for instance, choose as the first item to distribute the one where there is the greatest difference, amongst the parties, in perceived value).

There is a dynamic rating of issues based on who wins the item and who loses. The program will distribute items to the party who values them the most and compensates the other by giving them extra points for the next item. Other useful facilities could include:

- Provision of advice about trade-offs via decision support system—Adjusted Winner
- Provision of full ODR service
- Evaluation
- International abduction conflicts

3. Governance of Online Family Dispute Resolution Systems

Ebner and Zeleznikow (2016) compare the governance of Online Dispute Resolution Systems to the Wild West. They argue that there is minimal governance of how such systems operate or the advice they give. The issue of trust is of paramount importance. And in the family domain, trust is of even more importance. In many cases, the couples seeking out dispute resolution services will have ruptured relationships of trust among themselves, so they need to be able to have confidence in the system to which they present themselves. Who should parents trust, is a vital question:

- The Government,
- The Family Court,
- Non Government Organisations providing Family Dispute Resolution, or
- Private, for profit software providers.

1., 2., and 3. are important issues that will be discussed in later chapters.

References

Akin Ojelabi L (2010) Improving access to justice through alternative dispute resolution: the role of community legal centres in Victoria. Faculty of Law and Management, La Trobe University, Bundoora, Australia

Armstrong S (2010) Culturally responsive family dispute resolution in Family Relationship Centres: access and practice. Report for Family Relationship Centres at Bankstown, CatholicCare and Anglicare, Sydney

Bagshaw D (1999) Developing family mediation standards: an Australian experience. Confl Resolut Q 16:389–406

Barrett JT, Barrett J (2004) A history of alternative dispute resolution: the story of a political, social, and cultural movement. Jossey-Bass, San Francisco

Bellucci E, Zeleznikow J (2006) Developing Negotiation Decision Support Systems that support mediators: a case study of the Family_Winner system. J Artif Intell Law 13:233–271

Bibas S (2004) Plea bargaining outside the shadow of the trial. Harv Law Rev 117:2464–2547

Boyle KD (2013) A short history of family mediation in British Columbia. Paper prepared for Mediate BC Society. https://www.mediatebc.com/blog/a-short-history-of-family-mediation-in-british-columbia

Brown DG (1982) Divorce and family mediation: history, review, future directions. Concil Courts Rev 20:1–44

Brown HJ, Marriott AL (1999) ADR principles and practice, vol 13. Sweet & Maxwell, London

Casals MM (2005) Divorce mediation in Europe: an introductory outline. Electron J Comp Law 9:1–24

Casanovas P, Zeleznikow J (2014) Online dispute resolution and models of relational law and justice: a table of ethical principles. In: Casanovas P, Pagallo U, Sartor G, Ajani G (eds) AI approaches to the complexity of legal systems. Springer, Heidelberg, Berlin, pp 54–68

Casey T, Wilson-Evered E (2012) Predicting uptake of technology innovations in online family dispute resolution services: an application and extension of the UTAUT. Comput Hum Behav 28:2034–2045

Conley Tyler M, Bretherton D (2003) Developing an online mediation culture: the fourth generation of online ADR. Paper presented at the 2nd Asia Pacific Mediation Forum, Singapore, pp 1–19

Conley Tyler MH, McPherson MW (2006) Online dispute resolution and family disputes. J Fam Stud 12:165–183

Cooter R, Mark S, Mnookin R (1982) Bargaining in the shadow of the law: a testable model of strategic behavior. J Leg Stud 11:225–251

Crowe J, Toohey L (2009) From good intentions to ethical outcomes: the paramountcy of children's interests in the Family Law Act. Melb Univ Law Rev 33:391–414

Ebner N, Zeleznikow J (2016) No sheriff in town: governance for the ODR field. Negot J 32:297–323

Fletcher R (2008) Mothers and fathers accessing family relationship centres. Fam Relationships Q (Australian Institute of Family Studies) 10:3–5
French B (2007) Dispute resolution in Australia – the movement from litigation to mediation. Australas Disp Resolut J 18:213–221
Galanter M (2004) The vanishing trial: an examination of trials and related matters in state and federal courts. J Empir Leg Stud 1:459–570
González Martín N (2015) International parental child abduction and mediation. Anuario Mexicano de Derecho Internacional 15:353–412
Kaspiew R, De Maio J, Deblaquiere J, Horsfall B (2012) Evaluation of a pilot of legally assisted and supported family dispute resolution in family violence cases. Australian Institute of Family Studies, Melbourne. https://www.ag.gov.au/Publications/Documents/ArchivedFamilyLawPublications/CFDR%20Evaluation%20Final%20Report%20December%202012.PDF
Katsh E, Rifkin J (2001) Online dispute resolution: resolving conflicts in cyberspace. Jossey-Bass, San Francisco
Lodder A, Zeleznikow J (2010) Enhanced dispute resolution through the use of information technology. Cambridge University Press, Cambridge
McIntosh J, Burke S, Dour N, Gridley H (2009) Parenting after separation: a position statement prepared for The Australian Psychological Society. The Australian Psychological Society, Melbourne
Milne AL, Folberg J, Salem P (2004) Divorce and family mediation: models, techniques, and applications. Guilford Publications, NY
Mnookin R, Kornhauser L (1979) Bargaining in the shadow of the law: the case of divorce. Yale Law J 88:950–997
Nash J (1953) Two person cooperative games. Econometrica 21:128–140
National Alternative Dispute Resolution Advisory Council (2001) On-line ADR: background paper. Department of Finance and Administration, Canberra
Nicholson A, Harrison M (2000) Family law and the family court of Australia: experiences of the first 25 years. Melb Univ Law Rev 24:757–783
Pali B, Voet S (2013) Family mediation in international family conflicts: The European context. Leuven Institute of Criminology, Leuven
Parkinson P (2013) The idea of family relationship centres in Australia. Fam Court Rev 51:195–213
Pawlowski R (2007) Alternative dispute resolution for Hague Convention child custody disputes. Fam Court Rev 45:302–321
Sander F (1976) Varieties of dispute processing. Charted Institute of Arbitrators, London
Sourdin T, Liyanage C (2012) The promise and reality of online dispute resolution in Australia. In: Abdel Wahab MS, Katsh E, Rainey D (eds) Online dispute resolution: theory and practice. Eleven International Publishing, The Hague, pp 471–498
Spencer D, Hardy S (2014) Dispute resolution in Australia: cases, commentary and materials. Thomson Reuters, New South Wales
Sullivan PL (2005) Culture, divorce, and family mediation in Hong Kong. Fam Court Rev 43:109–123
Thomson M (2009) Annual report of the telephone dispute resolution service to the attorney general. Relationships Australia, Queensland
Thomson M (2011) Alternative modes of delivery for family dispute resolution: the Telephone Dispute Resolution Service and the online FDR project. J Fam Stud 17:253–2157
Wahab MSA, Katsh ME, Rainey D (2012) Online dispute resolution: theory and practice: a treatise on technology and dispute resolution. Eleven International Pub, Portland, OR
Wilson-Evered E, Macfarlane D, Zeleznikow J, Thomson M (2011) Towards an online family dispute resolution service in Australia. Mob Technol Confl Manag:125–138
Zdenek C (2014) The United States versus Japan as a lesson commending international mediation to secure Hague abduction convention compliance. San Diego Int Law J 16:209–261
Zeleznikow J (2014) Comparing the Israel – Palestinian dispute to Australian family mediation. Group Decis Negot J 23:1301–1317

Chapter 2
Artificial Intelligence and Online Family Dispute Resolution

Abstract The integration of technology with dispute resolution practices follows the identification of a range of value-added benefits in both formal and informal legal proceedings. In recent years, there has been a movement towards investigating how artificial intelligence (AI) can enhance the functioning of online family dispute resolution (OFDR) systems after successful application to other types of disputes. This chapter provides an overview of the development of AI in disputes in order to understand current progress within family law. Several existing negotiation support systems for use in Australian family contexts are described, including Split-Up, Family_Winner, and Asset-Divider, the latter of which incorporates principles of justice in a game theory framework. Negotiation support systems facilitate informed decision-making through performance improvement via machine learning while the integration of game theory assists in the distribution of resources to ensure the best outcome. As online dispute resolution begins to gain public and private traction culminating in the normalisation and institutionalisation of services, it becomes important to carefully consider issues of justice, regulation, and quality assurance.

2.1 Introduction

A decade and a half ago, Zeleznikow (2002) claimed that "The growing rise in the number of litigants who represent themselves in court has undesirable consequences for the administration of justice". He further claimed that "Thus it is important for us to investigate how the use of technology, especially artificial intelligence, the internet and Online Dispute Resolution can help the functioning of courts and provide better support for pro se litigants. Conducting such research will provide self-represented litigants with important knowledge as well as providing useable systems". He believed that the development of such systems will lead to:

E. Wilson-Evered, J. Zeleznikow, *Online Family Dispute Resolution*, Law, Governance and Technology Series 45,
https://doi.org/10.1007/978-3-030-64645-5_2

- Consistencies—by replicating the manner in which decisions are made, decision support systems are encouraging the spread of consistency in legal decision making.
- Transparency—by demonstrating how legal decisions are made, legal decision support systems are leading to better community understanding of legal domains. This has the desired benefit of decreasing the level of public criticism of judicial decision making.[1]
- Efficiency—one of the major benefits of decision support systems is to make courts and law firms more efficient.
- Enhanced support for dispute resolution—users of legal decision support systems are aware of the likely outcome of litigation (their BATNA[2]) and are thus encouraged to avoid the costs and emotional stress of legal proceedings.

The foundations of artificial intelligence (AI) can be attributed to early philosophers such as Aristotle and Plato who contemplated upon the human ability to think, know, and learn. It has since intrigued many to consider whether these seemingly unique human abilities could be replicated in an artificial environment (Luger 2002). In contemporary settings, this question continues to garner public interest through fantastical depictions in popular media and science fiction. However, the progress of, and interest in, AI technologies has waxed and waned across time (Bell 2019).

Turing (1950) initially stimulated attention in AI with his proposal of "The Imitation Game" (i.e., the Turing Test). This proposal remains today a perplexing problem that drives innovation through the postulation of a simple question: "Can machines think?". To provide evidence supporting this claim, the output of a machine would need to be virtually indistinguishable from human output as demonstrated through a blind test. No machine has yet proved itself worthy of such a deception. The 1950s also saw the first usage of the term 'artificial intelligence', attributed to John McCarthy during the 1956 Dartmouth College conference (Smith 2006).

Despite this promising start, innovation stagnated during the 1970s and 1980s in what has been described as the 'AI Winter'. Following several evaluations which reported minimal returns on government funding in AI advancement, financial support was reduced, and public interest decreased (Yang 2006). It was not until the 1990s that interest resurged, which coincided with the growth of the internet (OECD 2019). In 1995, the first AI computer program "Logic Theorist" was developed by Allen Newell and Herbert Simon and in 1997, "Deep Blue", a

[1]Judges of the Family Court of Australia are worried about criticism of the court, which has led to the death of judges and physical attacks on courtrooms. They believe enhanced community understanding of the decision-making process in Australian Family Law will lead to reduced conflict.

[2]Fisher and Ury (1981) introduced the idea of a BATNA as one's best alternative to a negotiated agreement. The reason you negotiate with someone is to produce better results than would otherwise occur. If you are unaware of what results you could obtain if the negotiations are unsuccessful, you run the risk of entering into an agreement that you would be better off rejecting; or rejecting an agreement you would be better off entering into.

chess-playing computer, won the first chess tournament against a world champion human opponent (OECD 2019). Simultaneous advancements and spread of technology has led to an increased usage of AI in everyday life (i.e., virtual assistants, machine learning, speech recognition, and self-driving vehicles).

For the past 30 years, Artificial Intelligence, Expert Systems, Case Based Reasoning and Machine Learning have been used by the legal profession, often in court related circumstances (Lodder and Zeleznikow 2010; Stranieri and Zeleznikow 2006; Zeleznikow and Hunter 1994). Zeleznikow and his research group at the Donald Berman Laboratory, Latrobe University, Melbourne, Australia, used a number of inferencing techniques in legal domains, including: association rules, case-based reasoning, machine learning, neural networks and rule induction. Domains investigated included: Workers Compensation (IKBALS), Credit Law (CAAS), Family Law Property Distribution (Split Up), Family Law Mediation (Asset Divider), Refugee Law (Embrace), Eligibility for Legal Aid (GetAid), Copyright Law (RightCopy), Eye-Witness Identification (ADVOKATE), Examining the causes of death (natural causes, suicide or homicide), Sentencing and the Building Industry.

Zeleznikow (2017) gives a detailed analysis of three systems his team has built:

1. GetAid (Stranieri and Zeleznikow 2002)—which provides advice on eligibility for Legal Aid in Victoria Australia
2. Split Up (Stranieri et al. 1999)—which gives advice on how to distribute property following separation in Australia; and
3. Asset Divider (Bellucci and Zeleznikow 2006)—which supports separating couples to perform trade-offs when distributing their property.

Only (3) provides direct support for dispute resolution. So why did it take two decades for developers (as distinct from researchers) to express an interest in using artificial intelligence for dispute resolution?

Intelligence can prove very useful when dealing with reasoning rather than transactions—a skill that is very important in courts. Lodder and Zeleznikow (2012) claim that "at the regularly organized UN Forums on ODR, the topic of Artificial Intelligence and Online Dispute Resolution has not been addressed very often".[3] In their 2005 Harvard Negotiation Law journal article they claim: "Artificial

[3]Exceptions included AR Lodder & EM Thiessen, 'The role of artificial intelligence in online dispute resolution', Proceedings of the UNECE Forum on ODR 2003 (http://www.odr.info/unece2003) and EM Thiessen & J Zeleznikow, 'Technical aspects of online dispute resolution - challenges and opportunities', Proceedings of the United Nations Annual Forum on Online Dispute Resolution 2004 (http://www.odr.info/unforum2004/thiessen_zeleznikow.htm). The authors of this chapter have been working on ODR topics for over 10 years now, but for approximately 20 years have also been active in the field of Artificial Intelligence and Law. For an introduction see AR Lodder & A Oskamp (eds.), Information Technology and Lawyers. Advanced Technology in the Legal Domain, from Challenges to Daily Routine, Springer. Moreover, the authors also initiated the ODR workshop series that have been held since 2003 in conjunction with either the International Conference on AI and Law, or the JURIX conferences. In particular the latter indicates there is quite some activity on the intersection of AI and ODR.

Intelligence involves the study of automated human intelligence. This includes both practically-oriented research, such as building computer applications that perform tasks requiring human intelligence, and fundamental research, such as determining how to represent knowledge in a computer-comprehensible form. At the intersection of Artificial Intelligence on the one hand and law on the other lies a field dedicated to the use of advanced computer technology for legal purposes: Artificial Intelligence and Law".

There are many advantages to integrating AI into the practice of law and justice that enable it to compensate for the weaknesses in human negotiation. Indeed, Luger (2002) provides a counterargument to contemporary efforts in designing AI to match and mimic human ability by suggesting that the unique capabilities of technology should be maximised to perhaps exceed human capacities. There have been a number of problems identified with human negotiation tactics that limit the potential for satisfactory outcomes, including: failure to recognize all alternatives; settling for less; making larger concessions than necessary; insufficient negotiation preparation; cognitive and logic errors; emotional reactions that impede optimal negotiation; being overwhelmed by the presence of multiple issues and parties (Hindriks and Jonker 2008; Thiessen and McMahon 2000).

This final point is particularly relevant to the field of family law where many issues are often in contention during the process of divorce settlement and child custody parenting plans. The human negotiation method of managing issues individually has been found to lead to suboptimal outcomes (Thiessen and McMahon 2000). The inclusion of AI in negotiation processes can assist in reducing the cognitive load of disputing parties by handling complexity with ease (Hindriks and Jonker 2008; Lopes et al. 2008; Thiessen and McMahon 2000). The mental effort required by third party intervenors may also be reduced through case-based reasoning technology, whereby a library of previous similar cases can be recalled to provide relevant solutions. Although mediators and lawyers can have a wealth of experiences and education to draw from, computing software does not suffer from the same limits to memory, storage, and retrieval (Bellucci and Zeleznikow 2001; Hindriks and Jonker 2008; Lodder and Zeleznikow 2012).

Technology can also help to improve communication between disputants by improving understanding of the process. Autonomy and agency can be somewhat restored to the litigant through AI-enhanced negotiation that provides education about their claims as well as the strengths and weaknesses of these claims, offers advice about their options through hypothetical simulations of their case and likely outcomes if presented before a court, and helps to select and communicate priorities in negotiation (Bell 2019; Bellucci and Zeleznikow 2006; Zeleznikow 2017).

Finally, AI has been argued to overcome the biases that are inherent in human negotiation. Notably, computers are free from the emotional reactions that may inhibit one from pursuing a fair outcome and procedure. Computers provide more objective, analytical, and rational responses (Alarie et al. 2017; Bellucci and Zeleznikow 2001). However, while technology may overcome the biases of the human negotiator, it would be a mistake to consider it completely value-neutral. Technology reflects the biases, values, and positions of the program developers who designed it (Bell 2019). With a mindful consideration of these caveats, AI can go 'beyond win-win' to deliver optimised negotiation outcomes (Thiessen and McMahon 2000).

Lodder and Zeleznikow (2010) produced a research monograph dedicated to the issue of the use of intelligent decision support systems to support dispute resolution. Whilst they do consider artificial intelligence and online family dispute resolution, much of their discussion does not revolve in online systems, let alone family dispute resolution. A 2012 chapter, (Lodder and Zeleznikow 2012) in an edited book with the title '*Online Dispute Resolution: Theory and Practice, A Treatise on Technology and Dispute Resolution*' does focus upon Artificial Intelligence and Dispute Resolution. It has some mention of the family domain.

2.2 Some Early Artificial Intelligence Systems That Provide Dispute Resolution Advice

Traditionally, negotiation support systems were template based, with little attention given to the role the system itself should play in negotiations and decision-making support. The primary role of these systems has been to demonstrate to users how close (or far) they are from a negotiated settlement. The systems do not specifically suggest solutions to users. However, by informing users of the issues in dispute and a measure of the level of the disagreement, they provide some decision support.

Eidelman (1993) discussed two template-based software systems that were available to help lawyers negotiate: *Negotiator Pro* and *The Art of Negotiating*. INSPIRE was initially a template-based negotiation support system that used utility functions to graph offers (Kersten 1997). It enabled disputants to negotiate through the Internet, making extensive use of email and web browser facilities. The system displayed previous and present offers and used utility functions to evaluate proposals determined to be Pareto-optimal.[4] Disputants communicated by exchanging offers and electronic mail and could check the closeness of a package to their initial preferences through a utility graph function.

The earliest negotiation support systems that used artificial intelligence were developed by the Rand Corporation in the early 1980s to advise upon risk assessment in damages claims. Lift Dispatching System (LDS) assisted legal experts in settling product liability cases (Waterman et al. 1986). LDS's knowledge consisted of legislation, case law and, importantly, informal principles and strategies used by lawyers and claims adjustors in settling cases.

NEGOPLAN is a rule-based system written in PROLOG (Matwin et al. 1989). It addresses a complex, two-party negotiation problem. Its method does not simulate the entire negotiation process. It gives one party a competitive advantage. The

[4]Pareto-optimality refers to a situation where at least one party is better off, without making other parties worse off.

opposing party's goals and subgoals are hidden from the side supported by NEGOPLAN. The opposing party reveals only those issues that are the subject of the bargaining. NEGOPLAN has been used to advise upon industrial disputes in the Canadian paper industry.

PERSUADER integrates case-based reasoning and game theory to provide decision support with regard to U.S. labor disputes (Sycara 1993). One of the crucial characteristics of negotiation support is systems that are capable of improving their performance, both in terms of efficiency and solution quality, by employing machine learning techniques. The model integrates case-based reasoning and decision theoretic techniques (multi-attribute utilities) to provide enhanced conflict resolution and negotiation support in group problem solving.

Artificial Intelligence and game theory[5] have often been used to support the resolution of international conflicts. MEDIATOR used case retrieval and adaptation[6] to propose solutions to international disputes. The MEDIATOR's task domain is common-sense advice giving for the resolution of resource disputes. GENIE integrates rule-based reasoning and multi-attribute analysis to advise upon international disputes (Wilkenfeld et al. 1995). It can aid crisis negotiators in identifying utility maximizing goals and in developing strategies to achieve these goals. GENIE provides the user with a strong set of tools which aid in the search for utility maximizing goals and strategies.

Kraus et al. (2008) present an automated agent that negotiates efficiently with human players in a simulated bilateral international crisis. The agent negotiates in a situation characterized by time constraints, deadlines, full information, and the possibility of opting out of negotiation. The specific scenario that they focus on concerns a crisis between Spain and Canada over access to a fishery in the North Atlantic. Canada blames Spain for over-fishing near its territorial waters and thereby damaging the flatfish stock.

There have attempts using game theory to use computer modelling to resolve international disputes. For example, Denoon and Brams (1997) have used the Adjusted Winner algorithm to advise upon the claims of China, Taiwan and four members of the Association of Southeast Asian Nations (ASEAN)—Vietnam, the Philippines, Malaysia, and Brunei to part or all of the land areas and surrounding waters of the Spratly Islands (a group of over 230 small islands and reefs in the South China Sea), which were believed to have major oil and gas deposits.

Adjusted Winner has also been applied to the Panama Canal treaty and Camp David Accords. Brams and Togman (1998) applied the Adjusted Winner procedure to the final status issues between Israel and the Palestinians.

[5]Game theory is a branch of applied mathematics that provides advice about the optimal distribution of resources. In the case of a negotiation, the goal of game theory is to develop the best outcome related to the choices each person has made.

[6]Case adaptation takes a retrieved case that meets most of the needs of the current case and turns it into one that meets all of the case's needs (Kolodner and Simpson 1989).

Zeleznikow (2014) used the game theoretic approach developed in his Asset Divider system (see later in this chapter) to propose resolutions for the Israeli-Palestinian dispute. The system suggested that

1. Israel recognise a Palestinian state, with East Jerusalem as its capital.
2. Israel dismantle the current security fence and evacuate those smaller settlements that are not in close proximity to current Israeli borders.
3. The Palestinians would need to recognise the State of Israel and encourage other Arab states to do likewise.
4. Palestinians would have to forgo any right of return to Israel (for which they would be compensated) and do their utmost to ensure no anti Israel activities emanated from Israeli territories.
5. Palestine would need to encourage Iran not to develop nuclear weapons and not to make belligerent statements against Israel.

Interestingly enough this is similar to the Camp David Accords between Israel and Egypt in 1978, where Israel returned certain territory for recognition and security. However, whilst the Camp David Accords have endured, the then Egyptian President Anwar Sadat, who signed the Accords, was assassinated by an Egyptian in 1981, and the Israeli Prime Minister Yitzhak Rabin, who signed the Oslo Accords in 1993, was assassinated by an Israeli in 1995. Clearly, any peace partner is at peril from dissidents on his own side.

What one can conclude from this research, is that the problem in the Israeli-Palestinian dispute is not the lack of any sensible solution that will equally meet the needs of both disputants. The major problem is that each party has no trust that their opponent will abide by such agreements. And of course the longer the conflict continues, the greater the mistrust!

2.3 Towards an Intelligent Online Family Dispute Resolution System

The term Online Dispute Resolution is used in various ways by different users. As Ebner and Zeleznikow (2016) state:

> The ODR field, since its genesis in the mid-1990s, has developed in bursts and spurts, largely because of ODR's connections to the areas of Internet development and e-commerce (Katsh 2012) and also because of the more general evolution of alternative dispute resolution (ADR) that has taken place in the last thirty years.
>
> At first, ODR seemed like an oddity or anomaly even in the eyes of ADR professionals. No more. As the field has grown and gained traction, it has received increasing attention from professional associations and industry leaders in the dispute resolution world. Even as ODR's status solidifies inside the ADR field, it has also increasingly received attention and recognition from sources outside this milieu. Signs of this are visible in both the private and public sectors.

> In the private sector, we see signs of ODR's expanding role across a number of fields. In the area of e-commerce, online dispute resolution's early and resounding success in resolving disputes at eBay and PayPal has not been duplicated elsewhere but the road is being paved for its utility for settling disputes originating in online reputation and feedback systems (such as customer reviews posted on Yelp.com or TripAdvisor.com) (Rule and Singh 2012). Beyond e-commerce, private-sector implementation of ODR has advanced in a variety of other areas. Online dispute resolution service providers have been targeting conflict niches and authors have offered suggestions for operationalizing ODR to resolve workplace disputes (Parlamis et al. 2016). More generally, private-sector mediators have started to offer online services as an add-on to their traditional, face-to-face practice (Ebner 2012).

Writing in 2004, Anita Ramasastry suggested that technology-assisted dispute resolution might have its most meaningful effects in contexts beyond the e-commerce arena and that it should be examined for its potential in the realm of government-to-citizen disputes. Today, this area is developing rapidly. One current initiative is Modria.com's tax assessment dispute settlement service, which has been adopted by several local government jurisdictions in the United States; this service enables property owners appealing property tax assessment to have their case reviewed and resolved through a combination of online and offline procedures (Ambrogi 2015). And recently Modria has been acquired by Tyler Technologies.[7]

American government agencies, including the National Mediation Board and the Office of Government Information Services, have somewhat adopted ODR processes (Katsh 2012), but the tax assessment appeals process goes beyond internalizing ODR for organizational communication and interaction, and constitutes the first case of institutionalization of ODR as a significant mode of providing governmental services to the public.

Indeed, over the past few years, other significant indicators of institutionalization have begun to emerge, with international and government agencies, and, more recently, court systems beginning to incorporate ODR. One early example of ODR institutionalization occurred in 1999 when the Internet Corporation for Assigned Names and Numbers (the non-profit that distributes Internet protocol addresses and domain names) adopted online arbitration as the resolution mechanism for all domain name disputes. This move wove ODR into the very fabric of Internet governance (Zweibel 2011). It took some time, however, before institutions unconcerned with Internet development took notice of ODR.

The United Nation's Commission on International Trade Law (UNCITRAL), charged with harmonizing commercial law to encourage international trade, began exploring the use of cross-border ODR in 2010; since 2012 it has been developing ODR Rules for disputes arising from e-commerce transactions (UNCITRAL 2016).

In 2013, two new dispute resolution regulations came into effect in the European Union (EU). The first, known as the ADR Directive, promotes the use of ADR for consumer disputes in general; the second, known as the ODR Regulations, creates a central ODR platform intended to promote use of ADR and ODR for cross-border

---

[7]See http://modria.com/blog/2017/05/30/modria-joins-forces-with-tyler-technologies/ last accessed 31 August 2017.

disputes concerning online transactions. Although it is too early to fully discuss the development of ADR and ODR though these mechanisms, they represent a new phase of institutionalization, recognition, and mainstreaming of ODR.[8]

In 2016, the Canadian province of British Columbia established its Civil Resolution Tribunal, an official branch of the court system that has jurisdiction over small claims, condominium disputes, societies and cooperative associations disputes, and motor vehicle injury claims. In this system, the first full integration of ODR into a formal court system, ODR, while voluntary, is the default and primary mechanism for settling disputes (for a discussion of previous and partial efforts, see Vermeys and Benyekhlef 2012).

Recently, countries without a strong history of online-supported mediation services have expressed an interest in growing their capacity to deliver ODR. Countries such as Japan (Habuka and Rule 2017), Brazil (Vierira de Carvalho Fernandes et al. 2018), Russia (Liubin 2018), Malaysia (Kamarudin et al. 2020), Kenya (Gachie 2016), Slovak Republic (Gábriš 2018), Vietnam (Thi Hong Nhung 2017), Pakistan (Khan et al. 2018), Indonesia (Yuniarti 2019), and India (Aamir Ali 2019) have acknowledged the benefits of ODR and, by learning from the implementation of previous international ODR services, they are considering the growth and regulation of their own within their unique cultural environments.

As the ODR field develops along a path from individual private-sector initiatives to widespread public sector institutionalization, observers and participants will undoubtedly raise questions about quality, ethics, practitioner training, service provider qualifications, and monitoring. In short, this attention will result in investigation of the field's governance.

As we can see, there are a variety of different Online Dispute Resolution Systems, often with very little in common. In 2004, Thiessen and Zeleznikow observed that Online Dispute Resolution Systems (ODR) can be classified into the following categories as indicated in Table 2.1. Additional process types have been developed in recent years which have also been included into Table 2.1 (Verma et al. 2018). The systems represent a wide range of approaches to dispute resolution (e.g., Artificial Intelligence, Social Psychology, and Game Theory). Given the wide variety of possibilities, it should be clear that there is no universally best approach or technique. Rather, there is an eclectic bag of methods with properties and performance characteristics that vary significantly depending on the context (Jennings et al. 2001).

What all of the selected ODR Systems have in common is that they provide an alternative to litigation providing a mechanism by which parties involved in a dispute can communicate over the Internet. Many of the illustrated systems are

---

[8]The ADR Directive (Directive 2013/11/EU of the European Parliament and of the Council of 21 May 2013 on alternative dispute resolution for consumer disputes) is available at eur-lex.europa.eu/LexUriServ/LexUriServ.do?uri=OJ:L:2013:165:0063:0079:EN:PDF The ODR Regulations (Directive 2013/11/EU of the European Parliament and of the Council of 21 May 2013 on alternative dispute resolution for consumer disputes) are available at eur-lex.europa.eu/LexUriServ/LexUriServ.do?uri=OJ:L:2013:165:0001:0012:EN:PDF.

Table 2.1 Categorization of ODR systems

Category	Methods	Main players
Information systems	Provision of information that parties can use to resolve their dispute	Scenario Builder Notgoodenough.org
Univariate blind bidding	Automation for single monetary issues	CyberSettle
Document management for negotiation	Facilitators working online and/or offline with parties making use of formal structured document management tools to help them create their contract	Negoisst
eNegotiation (or automated mediation) systems	Sophisticated optimization algorithms to generate optimal solutions for complex problems	Family_Winner Inspire SmartSettle
Customized for negotiation or mediation of a particular type of dispute	Automated negotiation with structured forms	eBay UPI SquareTrade
General virtual mediation rooms	Human mediators working online with parties making use of mediums such as email, instant messengers, telephone and discussion forums	ECODIR Mediation Room SquareTrade
Arbitration systems	Human arbitrators working online with parties making use of mediums such as email, instant messengers, telephone and discussion forums	Word and Bond
Agreement monitoring	Compliance-based tools that create a record of communication among parties	Our Family Wizard
Online courts	Virtual courtrooms utilized by judges to pass official judgements	eCourtroom
Community dispute resolution/ Crowd-sourced ODR	Individuals can seek dispute solutions from members of the public on online forums	Peopleclaim Agree Online

specialized to provide the best approach for a particular path to resolution. Table 2.1 shows the various possible paths.

One particularly influential OFDR program was Rechtwizjer (translated to 'Signpost to Justice'), a Dutch online divorce mediation service developed through a collaborative effort by the Hague Institute for Innovation of Law, Modria, and the Dutch Legal Aid Board (Bell 2019; Dijksterhuis 2019). The website was initially released in 2007 catering to a range of dispute types. In 2015, Version 2.0 had a narrowed focus on divorce disputes. The website was intended to be self-directed, whereby parties were provided the resources in order to have control over their separation outcomes. Parties moved through four stages in developing their divorce agreement: the couple independently submitted the details of their divorce preferences into the program, the program collated both sets of input and offered a solution that the parties could use to draft a divorce plan, an agreed divorce plan was then reviewed by a lawyer who could then approve the plan for presentation to the court. Disputing parties could seek mediator assistance if they were unable to independently come to an agreement. Rechtwizjer was terminated in 2017 due to financial difficulties. However, that same year, Uit Elkaar was released using the foundations of Rechtwizjer to continue to offer divorce mediation solutions.

The United States has been an influential force in the OFDR field with platforms such as Matterhorn ODR and Modria (Tyler Technologies) systematically changing the way that the courts and dispute resolution providers deliver services. Recently, The Institute for the Advancement of the American Legal System (IAALS) has drawn upon Rechtwijzer and the successful Canadian program MyLawBC to propose a conceptual pilot OFDR service throughout the U.S. (Kourlis et al. 2016). IAALS argued that the project is a timely venture due to the public turning away from court-involved solutions to disputes, and the inability to match attorney supply to litigant demand. The proposed 'Family Law Portal' is intended to provide a range of resources in facilitating self-led OFDR, with an integrated and holistic approach through connections with courts, family counsellors, rent assistance services, and domestic violence shelters.

In early 2006, Relationships Australia Queensland approached John Zeleznikow to pursue the possibility of developing an Australian Family Dispute Resolution System. They had seen the publicity about his Family Winner System[9] and sought his advice to build an online system. Such a system would extend the Telephone Dispute Resolution system they had recently developed (Thomson 2011).

The resulting Australian Online Family Dispute Resolution System has tried to emulate face-to-face ADR (Bellucci et al. 2010) rather than use the additional facilities offered by the development of the World Wide Web. For example, Thomson (2011) explains how the Australian Online Family Dispute Resolution emulates the services provided by Dispute Resolution practitioners based at 65 Family Relationship Centres. The designers assumed that traditional face-to-face mediation would work best in the online environment. The goal in the remainder of this chapter is to show how Artificial Intelligence can extend Online Family Dispute Resolution systems.

2.3.1 DEUS

In July 1996, Stranieri and Zeleznikow received much publicity for their Split-Up system (described in Sect. 2.3.2 of this Chapter). The London Daily Telegraph had heard about the system which provided advice about the distribution of marital property following divorce. At that time, Prince Charles and Princess Diana were formalising a divorce settlement. The London Daily Telegraph wanted Stranieri and Zeleznikow to run the Split-Up system on the Royal couple's case.

Stranieri and Zeleznikow listed many objections to doing so including:

1. The Royal couple were not subject to Australian law;

[9]See https://www.youtube.com/watch?v=YOZczuvrou4 last accessed August 31 2017.

2. The case was not a 'commonplace case'; and
3. The size of the pool is unknown.

But the Daily Telegraph persisted in their request and the researchers eventually relented. They ran the system on the data that the newspaper had given them. The software classified Princess Diana as a single mother who had lost her job and hence awarded her 70% of the Common Property.

This advice received much media attention. And these comments led to our subsequent interest in dispute resolution and negotiation. Since then, we have developed a number of decision support systems that support negotiation in Australian Family: DEUS (Zeleznikow et al. 1995), Split-Up (Stranieri et al. 1999), Family_Negotiator (Bellucci and Zeleznikow 1997), AdjustWinner (Bellucci and Zeleznikow 1998), Family_Winner (Bellucci and Zeleznikow 2006), Family_Mediator (Zeleznikow and Bellucci 2006) and AssetDivider (Bellucci 2008).

The first of these systems was DEUS, a template-based system that displays the level of disagreement, with respect to each item, between disputants. The model underpinning the program calculates the level of agreement and disagreement between the litigants' goals at any given time. The disputants reach a negotiated settlement when the difference between the goals is reduced to nil. DEUS does not provide advice or use Artificial Intelligence. But it is useful for gaining an understanding of what issues are in dispute and the extent of the dispute over these issues. It is thus an important first step in providing negotiation decision support.

2.3.2 *Split-Up and Family Dispute Resolution*

Lodder and Zeleznikow (2005) claimed that it is important that parties to a dispute be aware of the likely outcome of a dispute if a judicial decision is made. Split-Up provides advice on property distribution following divorce (Zeleznikow 2004). In developing Split-Up, Australian Family Law experts were used to identify factors pertinent to property distribution following separation. A data set of past cases was then fed to machine-learning programs.[10] In this way Split-Up learned the way in which judges weighed factors in past cases, without resorting to developing rules.[11]

In the Split-Up system, the relevant variables were structured as data and claim items in 35 separate arguments. The claim items of some arguments were the data items of others, resulting in a tree that culminated in the ultimate claim that indicated the percentage split of assets a judge would likely to award the husband. The tree of variables is illustrated in Fig. 2.1.

[10] Machine learning is that subsection of learning in which the artificial intelligence system attempts to learn automatically.

[11] A rule based expert system is a collection of rules of the form : IF <condition(s)> THEN <action>.

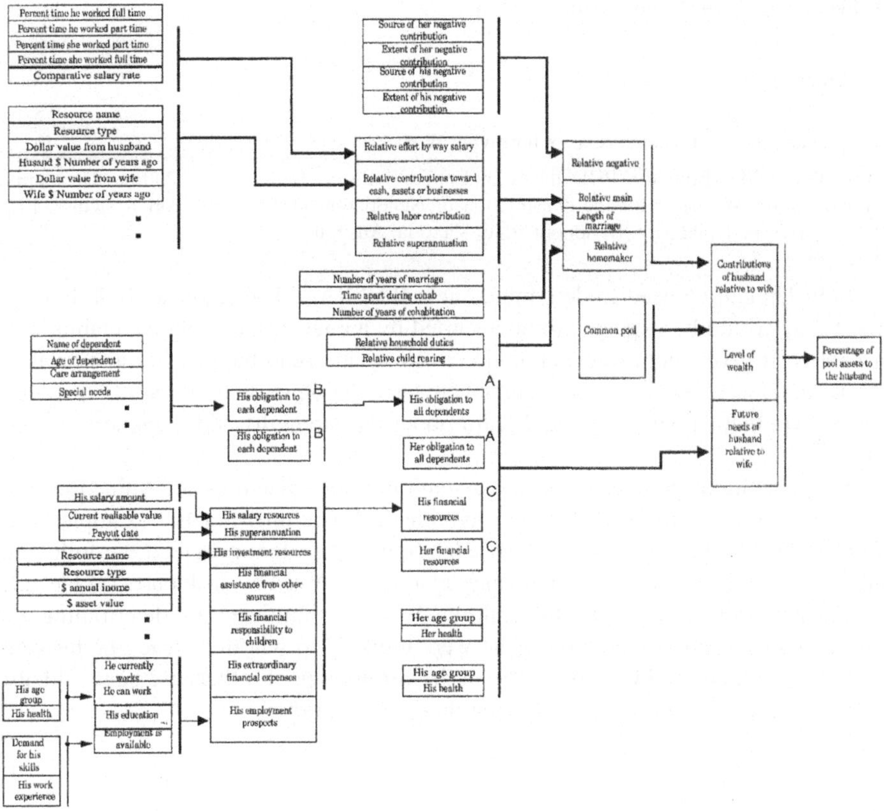

Fig. 2.1 Hierarchy of relevant factors for percentage split determination

In 15 of the 35 arguments, claim values were inferred from data items with the use of heuristics, whereas machine learning (in the form of neural networks) was used to infer claim values in the remaining 20 arguments. The neural networks were trained with data from only 103 commonplace cases.[12]

In consultation with domain experts, 94 variables were identified as relevant for the determination of a percentage split of the common pool. The way the factors combine was not elicited from experts as rules or complex formulas. Rather, values on the 94 variables were extracted from cases previously decided, so that a neural network could learn to mimic the way in which judges had combined variables. The relevant variables were structured as separate arguments following the argument structure advanced by Toulmin (1958).

[12]A commonplace case is one that does not provide any lessons by itself (as opposed to landmark cases), but together with numerous like cases can be used to derive conclusions.

Table 2.2 Split-Up example output

	W's %	H's %
Given one accepts W's beliefs	65	35
Given one accepts H's beliefs	42	58
Given one accepts H's beliefs except for giving W primary care of the children	60	40

This table comes from the PHD thesis of Emilia Bellucci: Bellucci, E. (2004), "Developing Compensation Strategies for the construction of Negotiation Decision Support Systems". PHD thesis, La Trobe University, Bundoora 3086, Victoria, Australia

Split-Up can be used to determine one's BATNA.[13] It first shows both litigants what they would be expected to be awarded by a court if their relative claims were accepted. It gives them relevant advice as to what would happen if some or all of their claims were rejected. Users are able to have dialogues with the Split-Up system about hypothetical situations and learn about the strengths and weakness of their claims.

Suppose the disputants' goals are entered into the system to determine the asset distributions for both W and H in a hypothetical example. For the example taken from Bellucci and Zeleznikow (2001), the Split-Up system provided the following answers as to the percentages of the marital assets received by each party (Table 2.2):

Clearly primary care of the children is very significant in determining the husband's property distribution. If he were unlikely to win this issue, the husband would be well advised to accept 40% of the common pool (otherwise he would also risk paying large legal fees and having ongoing conflict).

2.3.3 *Asset Divider and Game Theoretic Approaches to Family Dispute Resolution*

Family_Negotiator, AdjustWinner, Family_Winner, Family_Mediator and AssetDivider are all systems that use game theory to support disputing parties to conduct trade-offs in Australian Family Law. Each of them focus upon providing users with decision support on how they might best obtain their goals. Such advice is often based on Nash's principles of optimal negotiation or bargaining (Nash 1953).

Walton and Mckersie (1965) propose that negotiation processes can be classified as distributive or integrative. In distributive approaches, the problems are seen as *zero sum* and resources are imagined as fixed: *divide the pie.* In integrative approaches, problems are seen as having more potential solutions than are

---

[13]The word BATNA is an acronym for knowing. your best alternative to a negotiated agreement. The reason you negotiate with someone is to produce better results than would otherwise occur. If you are unaware of what results you could obtain if the negotiations are unsuccessful, you run the risk of entering into an agreement that you would be better off rejecting; or rejecting an agreement you would be better off entering into.

immediately obvious and the goal is to *expand the pie* before dividing it. Parties attempt to accommodate as many interests of each of the parties as possible, leading to the so-called *win-win* or *all gain* approach.

Family_Winner (Bellucci and Zeleznikow 2006) takes a common pool of items and distributes them between two parties based on the value of associated ratings. Each item is listed with two ratings (a rating is posted by each party), which signify the item's importance to the party. The algorithm to determine which items are allocated to whom works on the premise that each parties' ratings sum to 100; thereby forcing parties to set priorities. The basic premise of the system is that it allocates items based on whoever values them more.

Originally, the system was developed to meet clients' interests, with no concern for legal obligations. But as noted below, in Zeleznikow (2014), we incorporated principles of justice into the Asset-Divider system.

When evaluating the Family_Winner system, Bellucci and Zeleznikow (2006) were made aware of the limitations of using integrative negotiation for providing family mediation decision support. While both the evaluating solicitors and mediators were very impressed with the way Family_Winner suggested trade-offs and compromises, they had one major concern—that in focusing upon negotiation, the system had ignored the issues of justice. For example, Australian Family Law is based upon the paramount needs of the children rather than the interests of the parents. Thus a fair decision meets the needs of the children.

The AssetDivider system (Abrahams et al. 2012) incorporates the basis of Family_Winner's allocation and trade-off strategy to decide upon the allocation of assets based on interests and an item's monetary value. In a family property dispute one party may have a high emotional attachment to a record collection which has a minimal financial value.

AssetDivider accepts a list of items together with ratings (two per item) to indicate the item's importance to a party. In addition, it also accepts the current monetary value of each item in dispute. It is assumed that this dollar value has been negotiated (if necessary) before AssetDivider is used. Hence, only one-dollar value is entered per item. The proposed percentage split is also entered; this reflects what percentage of the common pool each party is likely to receive in the settlement.

AssetDivider's output consists of a list of items allocated to each party. All of the items (except one) on the allocation lists are provided in the intake screen by the disputants. The additional item is a "payout" item, which reflects the amount of money a disputant would need to pay the other party for the items they have been allocated. AssetDivider's allocation strategy works by allocating an item to the party whose rating is the highest i.e. to parties according to whoever values them the most. It then checks the dollar value of items it has been allocated previously (that is, their current list of items), the dollar value of the item presently allocated and the dollar amount permitted under the percentage split given by mediators. If by allocating the item in question the party exceeds its permitted amount, the item is removed from its allocation list and placed back into negotiation. In this case, the item has not been allocated to a party. If the dollar value of the item was within the limits of the amount permitted under the percentage split rule, then the allocation proceeds.

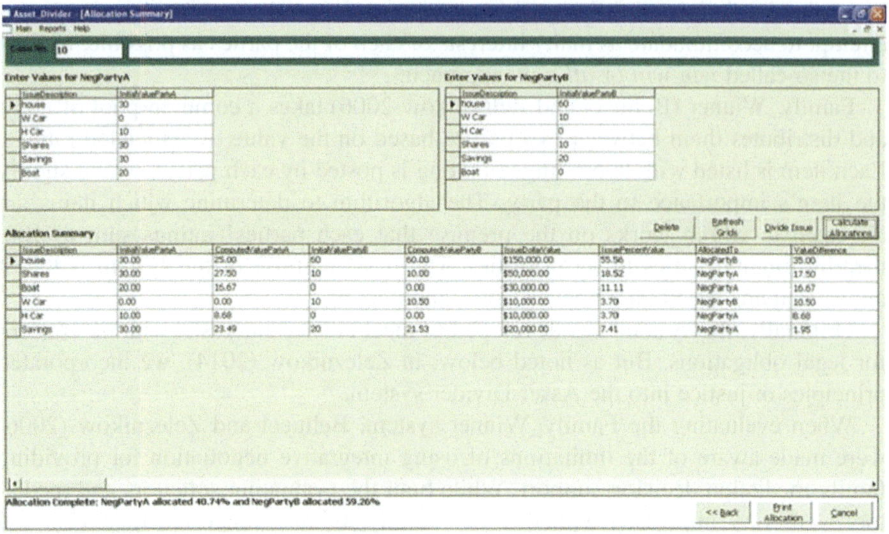

Fig. 2.2 Example use and output of AssetDivider. Reprinted by permission from Springer Nature: Springer Nature, Group Decision and Negotiation (Comparing the Israel—Palestinian dispute to Australian family mediation, Zeleznikow, J.), Copyright (2014)

Once an item has been allocated to a party, the remaining ratings (of items still in dispute) are modified by trade-off equations. These modifications try to mimic the effect losing or gaining an item will have on the rest of the items still in dispute.

The equations directly modify ratings by comparing each one against that of the item recently lost or won (each party's set of ratings are modified as a result of an allocation). The equations update ratings based on a number of variables—whether the item allocated was lost or gained, the value of the allocated item in relation to items still in dispute and the value of the item whose rating will change as a result. Only the 'losing party' in AssetDivider is compensated by modifying the trade-off equations.

An example of AssetDivider's output (Zeleznikow 2014) is (Fig. 2.2)

As has been demonstrated in this chapter, there currently exists several family and non-family related ODR systems available in Australia. This field is only expected to expand in the coming years as the technology becomes more accessible and public awareness of the benefits of engaging with technology-enhanced services for dispute resolution increases. For an in-depth understanding of what these benefits entail, and what guide-posts current systems can offer to future developments, a review of the research and practice into OFDR is considered timely. The following chapter presents the finding of such an investigation.

References

Aamir Ali SM (2019) Online dispute resolution: an emerging tool of dispute resolution in contemporary era. J Gujarat Res Soc 21:480–487

Abrahams B, Bellucci E, Zeleznikow J (2012) Incorporating fairness into development of an integrated multi-agent online dispute resolution environment. Group Decis Negot 21:3–28

Alarie B, Niblett A, Yoon A (2017) How artificial intelligence will affect the practice of law. Univ Toronto Law J 68:106–124

Ambrogi R (2015) Tax boards use an online system to resolve disputes. ABA J. www.abajournal.com/magazine/article/tax_boards_use_an_online_system_to_resolve_disputes/

Bell F (2019) Family law, access to justice, and automation. Macquarie Law J 19:103–132

Bellucci E (2008) AssetDivider: a new mediation tool in Australian family law'. In: Proceedings of the 1st International Working Conference on Human Factors and Computational Models in Negotiation, Delft, Netherlands, ACM 8–9 December, pp 11–18

Bellucci E, Zeleznikow J (1997) Family—Negotiator: an intelligent decision support system for negotiation in Australian Family Law. In: Proceedings of the Fourth Conference of the International Society for Decision Support Systems, Lausanne, pp 359–373

Bellucci E, Zeleznikow J (1998) A comparative study of negotiation decision support systems. In: Proceedings of the Thirty-First Hawaii International Conference on System Sciences, IEEE Computer Society, Los Alamitos, CA 6–9 January pp 254–256

Bellucci E, Zeleznikow J (2001) Representations of decision-making support in negotiation. J Decision Sys 10:449–479

Bellucci E, Zeleznikow J (2006) Developing negotiation decision support systems that support mediators: a case study of the family_winner system. J Artificial Intell Law 13:233–271

Bellucci E, Macfarlane D, Zeleznikow J (2010) How information technology can support family law and mediation. In: Proceedings of the International Conference on Business Information Systems, Heirdelberg, Berlin, 3–5 May, pp 243–255

Brams SJ, Togman TM (1998) Camp David: was the agreement fair? In: Harvey FP, Mor BD (eds) New directions in the study of conflict, crisis and war. Macmillan, London, pp 306–323

Denoon D, Brams S (1997) Fair division: a new approach to the Spratly Islands controversy. Int Negot 2:303–329

Dijksterhuis B (2019) The online divorce resolution tool '**Rechtwijzer** uit Elkaar' examined. In: Maclean M, Dijksterhuis B (eds) Digital family justice: from alternative dispute resolution to online dispute resolution? Bloomsbury Publishing Plc, Oxford, pp 193–214

Ebner N (2012) E-mediation. In: Abdel Wahab MS, Katsh E, Rainey D (eds) Online dispute resolution: theory and practice. Eleven International Publishing, The Hague, pp 369–398

Ebner N, Zeleznikow J (2016) No sheriff in town: governance for the ODR field. Negot J 32:297–323

Eidelman JA (1993) Software for negotiations. Law Prac Manag 19:50–55

Fisher R, Ury W (1981) Getting to yes: how to negotiate without giving in. Arrow, London

Gábriš T (2018) Heading towards online dispute resolution in the Slovak Republic. Hungarian J Legal Stud 59:74–94

Gachie AJ (2016) An evaluation of the need for regulation of online dispute resolution (ODR) in Kenya. Unpublished thesis for the University of Nairobi

Habuka H, Rule C (2017) The promise and potential of online dispute resolution in Japan. Int J Online Disp Resol 4:74–90

Hindriks KV, Jonker CM (2008) Creating human-machine synergy in negotiation support systems: towards the Pocket Negotiator. In: Proceedings of the 1st International working conference on human factors and computational models in negotiation, Delft, Netherlands, ACM 8–9 December, pp 47–54

Jennings NR, Faratin P, Lomuscio AR, Parsons S, Wooldridge M, Sierra C (2001) Automated negotiation: prospects, methods and challenges. Group Decis Negot 10:199–215

Kamarudin Z, Ilham Abdul Manaf Z, Kadir NA (2020) The necessity for the formulation of an online family dispute resolution management framework in Malaysia. J Inf Syst Digital Technol 2:1–15
Katsh E (2012) ODR: a look at history. In: Abdel Wahab MS, Katsh E, Rainey D (eds) Online dispute resolution: theory and practice. Eleven International Publishing, The Hague, pp 21–33
Kersten GE (1997) Support for group decisions and negotiations: an overview. In: Climaco J (ed) Multiple criteria decision making and support. Springer, Heidelberg, pp 332–346
Khan MD, Kaya S, Habib RI (2018) Global trends of online dispute resolution (ODR) with reference to online trade in Pakistan. Rev Econ Dev Stud 4:303–311
Kolodner JL, Simpson LR (1989) The mediator: analysis of an early case-based problem solver. Cogn Sci 13:507–549
Kourlis RL, Knowlton NA, Cornett L (2016) A court compass for litigants. Report prepared for the Institute for the Advancement of the American Legal System.
Kraus S, Hoz-Weiss P, Wilkenfeld J, Andersen DR, Pate A (2008) Resolving crises through automated bilateral negotiations. Artificial Intell J 172:1–18
Liubin I (2018) Online dispute resolution in Russia and Europe - Current situation and prospects of development. Paper presented at the 31st International Scientific conference on economic and social development - "Legal Challenges of Modern World", pp 197–203
Lodder AR, Zeleznikow J (2005) Developing an online dispute resolution environment: dialogue tools and negotiation systems in a Three Step Model. Harv Negot Law Rev 10:287–338
Lodder AR, Zeleznikow J (2010) Enhanced dispute resolution through the use of information technology. Cambridge University Press, Cambridge
Lodder AR, Zeleznikow J (2012) Artificial intelligence and online dispute resolution. In: Wahab M, Katsh E, Rainey D (eds) Online dispute resolution: theory and practice. Eleven International Publishers, Ten Haag, pp 61–82
Lopes F, Wooldridge M, Novais AQ (2008) Negotiation among autonomous computational agents: principles, analysis and challenges. Artificial Intell Rev 29:1–44
Luger G (2002) Artificial intelligence: structures and strategies for complex problem-solving, 4th edn. Addison Wesley, Massachusetts
Matwin S, Szpakowicz S, Koperczak Z, Kersten GE, Michalowski W (1989) NEGOPLAN: an expert system shell for negotiation support. IEEE Expert 4:50–62
Nash J (1953) Two-person cooperative games. Econometrica: J Econometric Soc 21:128–140
OECD (2019) Artificial intelligence in society. OECD Publishing, Paris
Parlamis J, Ebner N, Mitchell L (2016) Looking back to leap forward: the potential for e-mediation at work. In: Bollen K, Euwema M, Munduate L (eds) Advancing workplace mediation through integration of theory and practice. Springer, Houten, pp 233–249
Ramasastry A (2004) Government-to-citizen online dispute resolution: a preliminary inquiry. Wash Law Rev 79:159–174
Rule C, Singh H (2012) ODR and online reputation systems: maintaining trust and accuracy through online redress. In: Abdel Wahab MS, Katsh E, Rainey D (eds) Online dispute resolution: theory and practice. Eleven International Publishing, The Hague, pp 175–196
Smith C (2006) Introduction. In: The history of artificial intelligence. University of Washington, Seattle, pp 4–9
Stranieri A, Zeleznikow J (2002) WebShell: the development of web based expert systems. In: Bramer M, Coenen F, Preece A (eds) Research and development in intelligent systems XVIII. Springer, London, pp 245–258
Stranieri A, Zeleznikow J (2006) Knowledge discovery from legal databases, vol 69. Springer Science & Business Media, Berlin
Stranieri A, Zeleznikow J, Gawler M, Lewis B (1999) A hybrid rule- neutral approach for the automation of legal reasoning in the discretionary domain of family law in Australia. Artificial Intell Law 7:153–183
Sycara K (1993) Machine learning for intelligent support of conflict resolution. Decis Support Sys 10:121–136

Thi Hong Nhung N (2017) Online dispute resolution – experience for Vietnam. Paper presented at the International Conference for Young Researchers in Economics and Business Proceedings, Da Nang, Vietnam, pp 334–337

Thiessen EM, McMahon JP (2000) Beyond win-win in cyberspace. Ohio State J Disp Resol 15:643–667

Thiessen E, Zeleznikow J (2004) Technical aspects of online dispute resolution challenges and opportunities. In: Conley Tyler M, Katsh E, Choi D (eds) Proceedings of the third annual forum on online dispute resolution, Melbourne, Australia, 5–6 July

Thomson M (2011) Alternative modes of delivery for family dispute resolution: the telephone dispute resolution service and the online FDR project. J Family Stud 17:253–2157

Toulmin S (1958) The uses of argument. Cambridge University Press, Cambridge

Turing A (1950) Computing machinery and intelligence. In: Parsing the turing test. Springer, Dordrecht, pp 23–65

UNCITRAL (2016) Online working group III: online dispute resolution. www.uncitral.org/uncitral/commission/working_groups/3Online_Dispute_Resolution.html

Verma D, Banwari A, Pande N (2018) Online dispute resolution. In: Peña-Acuña B (ed) Digital communication management. IntechOpen, London, pp 139–149. https://doi.org/10.5772/intechopen.76032

Vermeys NW, Benyekhlef K (2012) ODR and the courts. In: Abdel Wahab MS, Katsh E, Rainey D (eds) Online dispute resolution: theory and practice. Eleven International Publishing, The Hague, pp 307–324

Vierira de Carvalho Fernandes R, Rule C, Tiemi Ono T, Estevam Botelho Cardoso G (2018) The expansion of online dispute resolution in Brazil. Int J Court Admin 9:20–31

Walton RE, McKersie RB (1965) A behavioral theory of labor negotiations. McGraw-Hill, New York

Waterman DA, Paul J, Peterson M (1986) Expert systems for legal decision making. Expert Syst 3:212–226

Wilkenfeld J, Kraus S, Holley KM, Harris MA (1995) GENIE: a decision support system for crisis negotiations. Decis Support Syst 14:369–391

Yang G (2006) AI winter and its lessons. In: The history of artificial intelligence. University of Washington, Seattle, pp 17–21

Yuniarti S (2019) Online dispute resolution as future dispute settlement in Indonesia. Paper presented at the WoMELA-GG 2019, January 26–28, Medan, Indonesia

Zeleznikow J (2002) Using web-based legal decision support systems to improve access to justice. Inf Commun Technol Law 11:15–33

Zeleznikow J (2004) The split-up project: induction, context and knowledge discovery in law. Law Prob Risk 3:147–168

Zeleznikow J (2014) Comparing the Israel – Palestinian dispute to Australian family mediation. Group Decis Negot J 23:1301–1317

Zeleznikow J (2017) Can artificial intelligence and online dispute resolution enhance efficiency and effectiveness in courts. Int J Court Admin 8:30–45

Zeleznikow J, Bellucci E (2006) Family_mediator- adding notions of fairness to those of interests. Front Artif Intell Appl 152:121–130

Zeleznikow J, Hunter D (1994) Building intelligent legal information systems: representation and reasoning in law. Kluwer Law and Taxation Publishers, Boston

Zeleznikow J, Meersman R, Hunter D, van Helvoort E (1995) Computer tools for aiding legal negotiation. Paper presented at the ACIS95 — Sixth Australasian Conference on Information Systems, Curtin University of Technology, Perth, Western Australia, 26–29 September, pp 231–251

Zweibel E (2011) Online dispute resolution. In: Macfarlane J (ed) Dispute resolution, 3rd edn. Emond Montgomery, Toronto

References

Chapter 3
Current Research and Practice in Online Family Dispute Resolution

Abstract The growth of Online Family Dispute Resolution (OFDR) means that consumers are now presented with a range of options on the market to suit their needs. With the intention of these services to optimise effectiveness and efficiency for their users, it is paramount that robust evidence be demonstrated for their quality to support their preferential use when compared to other forms of dispute resolution service delivery. The literature review presented in this chapter was conducted to scope the current research and practice evidence for online dispute resolution in family law as relating to child custody issues. The use of OFDR services in both Australian and international contexts was investigated across a range of electronic sources since 2011. Of those programs located by the review, it was evident that while more methodologically rigorous research is required, preliminary evidence shows support for OFDR effectiveness in reaching desirable and fair outcomes. The considerations for selecting technologically-enhanced services are discussed, as are the avenues for future research and directions to further develop OFDR as a viable option for informal conflict resolution. This chapter demonstrates how knowing the literature helps to inform future OFDR development and enhance service delivery.

3.1 Introduction

The fast-advancing field of technology in the twenty-first century has meant that interest in and the development of online dispute resolution (ODR) systems has grown exponentially since the concept was first developed in 1996. This unprecedented growth means that best-practices for the creation and use of online services are constantly being updated to reflect new knowledges. As it is critical that new technologies are informed by evidence-based research to ensure ethical processes and effective outcomes, there is a need to take stock and assess the current state of knowledge as it pertains to technological use in dispute resolution services. Further, the application of flexible and innovative service delivery options to family law has occurred fairly recently as compared to ODR's beginnings in e-commerce, which necessitates a review of recent progress in the field.

E. Wilson-Evered, J. Zeleznikow, *Online Family Dispute Resolution*, Law, Governance and Technology Series 45,
https://doi.org/10.1007/978-3-030-64645-5_3

The present review was conducted in August and September 2018 and was intended to contribute to an understanding of the current research and practice of OFDR in both Australian and international contexts. Future developments of OFDR services are grounded in the foundations of earlier developments and the lessons learned from such endeavours. As such, by compiling existing evidence, recommendations, and acquired knowledges over time, this review demonstrates not only the benefits of adopting online technologies into one's FDR practice, but also outlines the considerations for future innovation in this area.

This chapter will first outline the method and search strategy used to locate, screen, and analyse the literature on current uses of technologies to enhance family dispute resolution (FDR) service delivery. Common themes, learnings, and practices will then be extracted from the literature and presented to demonstrate the current state of OFDR practice and the potential areas for future service development. Finally, the results of a brief review of existing ODR and related services will be discussed to elucidate trends in how technologies are used.

3.2 Method

Existing Reviews A thorough search was conducted to locate any existing systematic reviews on OFDR and associated concepts. As no records appeared relevant to the field of investigation, it can be assumed that the current literature review is a novelty in this area of research within the specified search parameters.

3.2.1 Search Strategy

Although guided by systematic methods for data searching, processing, and extraction, the current literature review is not purely systematic due to resource limitations and the inadequate availability of empirical data in this field.

A wide range of electronic sources were targeted for the review to reflect the interdisciplinary nature of the topic, with databases, journals, and conference proceedings chosen that covered technology, psychology, law, and social sciences. In addition, attempts to locate grey literature were conducted, as well as the manual searching of ODR-related blogs. Finally, seminal texts on OFDR were forward-cited using Google Scholar and, where appropriate, the reference lists were manually searched.

For database searching, the following search string was developed and subsequently adapted to fit different requirements:

> tech* OR internet OR online OR on-line OR phone AND family AND ("conflict resolution" OR "mediation" OR "dispute resolution" OR "conflict management" OR "border abduction" OR "family dispute resolution" OR "family law" OR "child custody")

Where a search string was not required, the titles of the records were screened for relevance. All database entries were imported into EndNote X8.

Inclusion Criteria To be considered eligible for inclusion in the current review, records needed to be published between 2011 and 2018 with the lower limit reflecting the last comprehensive review conducted on OFDR. As the objective of the review was to investigate the use of OFDR internationally, English restrictions were not applied at this stage.

Regarding content, a record was considered appropriate for inclusion if it related to or made mention of: family law, online dispute resolution, online family dispute resolution, acceptance and uptake of technology for dispute resolution, family dispute resolution using technological tools, and/or child custody. Additional inclusion criteria—which were not directly related to OFDR but had bearings on its practice—included: training in ODR platforms, online meetings or therapy for separating parents, and/or online divorce education programs.

In addition, well-known papers published prior to 2011, and more general ODR papers (which did discuss Family Dispute Resolution) were also examined but did not comprise the basis of the literature review.

3.2.2 Search Results

The results of the search were examined with reference to PRISMA guidelines (see Fig. 3.1 for the PRISMA flow diagram). One research assistant reviewed the articles for relevance and sought second opinions from the authors when relevance was uncertain. The search strategy yielded a total of 2411 records. After the removal of duplicate records ($n = 394$), 2017 records remained. A further 1981 records were excluded after title and abstract screening revealed irrelevance according to the outlined inclusion and exclusion criteria. Of these records, 42 were not in English. Efforts were made to obtain translations of these records via Google Translate services, with four records unable to be translated, four appearing relevant from the title and/or abstract but the translation was of poor quality, and 34 not meeting inclusion criteria. Therefore, no non-English records were accepted for full-text review. At this final screening stage, an additional 15 records were removed due to duplicate content ($n = 3$), inadequate focus on OFDR ($n = 4$), outdated literature cited ($n = 3$), assets or property-based FDR ($n = 3$), or legal cases ($n = 2$).

At the conclusion of the screening process, 21 records were located for analysis. However, three of these articles (Araszkiewicz et al. (2013, 2014, 2015 [with Zurek]) were not independent (that is, the same authors present very similar content) and are considered as a 'single paper'. The final 19 records consisted of seven empirical studies (Becher et al. 2015; Bollen et al. 2014; Casey and Wilson-Evered 2012; Cronin et al. 2017; Gramatikov and Klaming 2012; Schramm and McCaulley 2012; Tait 2013), eight discussion papers (Augar and Zeleznikow 2014; Barsky 2016; Brennan 2011; González Martín 2015; LaMarca 2012; Lavi 2014; Rossi et al. 2017;

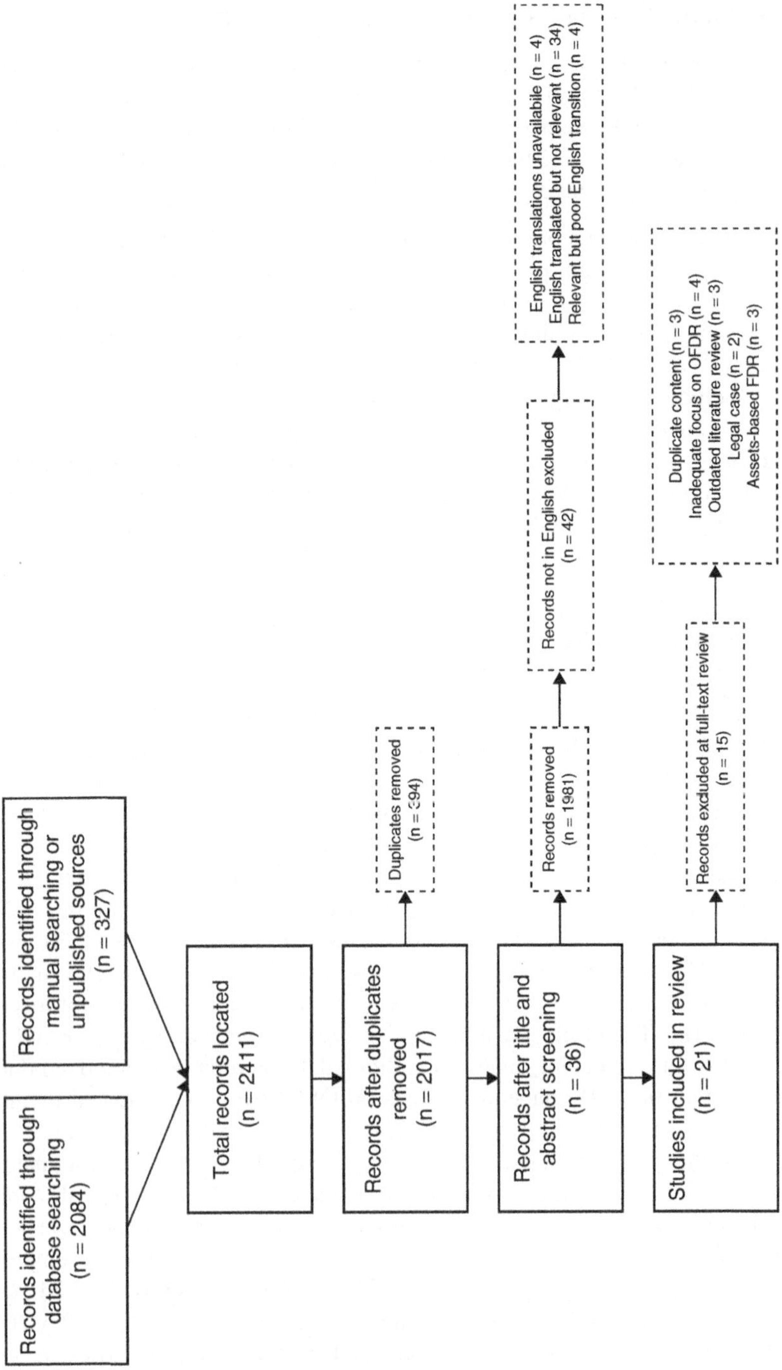

Fig. 3.1 OFDR literature search PRISMA flow diagram

Thomson 2011) two reviews of OFDR programs and services (Bowers et al. 2011; Knight and Hunter 2013), one proposal for a new OFDR system (Araszkiewicz et al. 2013, 2014, 2015), and one set of practice guidelines (Jani 2012). Significant ODR papers that also considered family Dispute Resolution were also considered. These included Lodder and Zeleznikow (2005), Bellucci and Zeleznikow (2006), Lodder and Zeleznikow (2010), Zeleznikow (2011, 2014) and Zeleznikow and Bellucci (2012).

Data Analysis The quality of the empirical studies was assessed using the Effective Public Health Practice Project Quality Assessment Tool for Quantitative Studies as all were quantitative, excluding Tait (2013) which was mixed-method. The results revealed weak quality because they lacked randomised controlled trials and thorough and transparent methodological reporting. Despite the low quality reported, the decision was made not to remove any records on the basis of quality assessment as there would be no records left for analysis.

Due to the large variation in resource type and content, no consistent data analysis approach was applied. Instead, themes were observed throughout the records and will be discussed in the remainder of the chapter.

3.3 Results

Differences by Location In terms of geographical location, the majority ($n = 8$) discussed ODR services in the United States (with one also citing examples from Mexico), four in Australia, two in Canada, two in the Netherlands, one in Poland, and two were unable to be determined. Although the sample size is not large enough to support confident conclusions, there were minimal differences observed across international OFDR applications. The main differences tended to be legal, with regards to the different laws in each country around child welfare and the family court. However, most studies that mentioned legal procedures emphasised that the court, mediators, and any developed programs should always work in the best interest of the child, over and above the parents' interests. While most programs also note that parents' interests should also be considered in any negotiations and child welfare decisions, Araszkiewicz et al. (2013, 2014, 2015) go further to argue additional consideration of the society in general, noting that decisions on how to raise a child will ultimately affect how they function as a member of society; however this may be idiosyncratic to Polish law.

The Araszkiewicz et al. papers and Zeleznikow papers prioritise the child's wellbeing. Araszkiewicz et al. present the conceptual framework for the Parent Plan Support System (PPSS), an online platform intended to assist separating parents residing in Poland who both want primary residency of their child(ren). The PPSS was developed to address a gap between the law and practice, such that Polish law requires parents to construct and submit a document outlining all possible parenting arrangements concerning the child (e.g., contact between parents and child, decisions on the child's education, decisions regarding holiday celebrations, how documentation and information about the child will be shared between parents). The authors noted that the law provided no guidance in how to structure this document, which might exacerbate conflict and negative emotions between parents in the subsequent struggle to develop a document that met the standards of the court. As such, the PPSS was proposed to provide a template and support for parents as they develop the plan. What is unique about the Polish context, however, is that the court assesses and approves the parenting plan by comparing it to the highest guiding principle: does this facilitate the child's wellbeing?

Program and Services Online tools were used for a variety of programs and services for family dispute resolution and family-related issues. There were tools to assist in drafting legal divorce documents (i.e., the Parent Plan Support System; Araszkiewicz et al. 2013, 2014, 2015), online mediation services (Bollen et al. 2014; Gramatikov and Klaming 2012; Lavi 2014; Rossi et al. 2017; Tait 2013; Thomson 2011), online counselling services (Augar and Zeleznikow 2014; *MoodGYM,* Knight and Hunter 2013), co-parenting apps (*mymob*, Knight and Hunter 2013), virtual visitation arrangements to connect non-custodial parents with their children (LaMarca 2012), pre-mediation programs (Augar and Zeleznikow 2014), informative websites and resources (*Raising Children Network*, Knight and Hunter 2013), and divorce education programs (Becher et al. 2015; Bowers et al. 2011; Cronin et al. 2017; Schramm and McCaulley 2012).

Of particular interest is this last category, in which Bowers et al. (2011) tested and reviewed six online divorce education programs in terms of their content, design, and teaching methods. They found that these programs (which were not named) varied in duration, taking between 2 h and 12 h to complete. They also found that while all programs appeared to be developed according to theoretical frameworks and empirical research, this content was seldom cited. This finding is in violation of Augar and Zeleznikow's (2014) recommendations that online programs and services need to provide evidence of the quality and validity of the information that they are presenting in order to facilitate trust in the resource. Consistent with laws and best practice guidelines stating that decisions regarding and affecting the wellbeing of children should be made by prioritising their wellbeing, all programs in the Bowers et al. review were child-focused. There was additional, albeit comparatively less, focus on parent-related and court-related content. In terms of the design, the authors reported poor accommodation to different audiences and learning needs (in terms of low accessibility and high reading levels) as well as passive teaching styles. They therefore recommend the use of more active and engaging strategies, more focus on specialised cases (i.e., domestic violence), and more content educating parents about legal processes.

As a final observation, the programs included in this review tended to be brief, one-off sessions. Only two conducted follow-up testing (Becher et al. 2015 and Cronin et al. 2017); however, this procedure was for the benefit of evaluation and did not include any additional skill training. Cronin et al. (2017) argue the need for 'booster' sessions that help to consolidate information and newly learned skills.

Effectiveness of OFDR Although the poor quality of the studies identified by the search strategy means that strong conclusions cannot be claimed, the findings do provide some evidence on the effectiveness of using online methods for family disputes. In the evaluation of MediateBC's *Distance Mediation Project Phase III*, Tait (2013) found that 85% of the cases completed (of which there were 46) ended in settlement, with higher settlements reported for cases that used videoconferencing tools in their mediation sessions (88%) compared to those cases that used telephone tools (80%). Clients also reported that they were satisfied with both the outcome (59%) and the process (70%) while mediators reported that ODR was more effective than shuttle mediation. Bollen et al. (2014) found similar settlement rates (84%) for their study on a pilot online divorce mediation program while Gramatikov and Klaming (2012) found slightly lower settlement rates (76%) for their pilot online divorce mediation program.

One study that examined the effectiveness of the *Parents Forever* online divorce education program reported decreases in parental conflict, increases in parental coping ability, and increases in controlling negative communication with the co-parent (Becher et al. 2015) at a 6-month follow-up. However, the second study that assessed *Parents Forever* 2 years later (Cronin et al. 2017) reported that 40% of parents experienced increases in conflict at the 6-month follow up, and that while decreases in conflict were associated with decreased negative co-parenting behaviours, it was also associated with decreases in positive co-parenting behaviour.

In only one study was the online program compared for effectiveness against an equivalent face-to-face program. Schramm and McCaulley (2012) found a single significant difference between participants' experiences of the online and the face-to-face *Focus on Kids* divorce education program; this difference being that the latter was reported as more worthwhile. Across both formats, there was high agreement that the program affected behavioural intentions and increased knowledge and skills in supporting children through the divorce process.

Suitability of Cases for OFDR The literature provides some recommendations for what cases are considered most appropriate for management by ODR process. Tait (2013) recommends that thorough screening can help to determine suitability, as disputes must be assessed on a case-by-case basis. Mediators Tait, in her evaluation of the Distance Mediation Project identified the following criteria for assessing suitability: parties' and mediator's level of comfort and proficiency with technology; domestic violence presence (severity, whether it is ongoing, whether parties will feel equal in mediation, the geographical proximity between the parties and between the parties and the mediator, whether technology was used to enable violent behaviour), case complexity, and cooperation of parties. Tait did find that level of conflict was not a factor in suitability assessments, such that both low and high conflict cases seemed to benefit from technology-enhanced mediation. Jani (2012) recommends that this assessment should not be limited to intake sessions and that instead mediators should remain vigilant and constantly monitor the suitability of the platform for the case and the parties in question.

Advantages of OFDR As many of the records were discussion papers, there was some overlap in content regarding the advantages and disadvantages of OFDR. Many were citations of other research (that were not followed up in the current literature review as they fell outside of the publication year inclusion range), however some (Tait 2013) provided primary sources of data. Identified benefits for using online rather than face-to-face methods for dispute resolution include: options for asynchronous and synchronous communication (Araszkiewicz et al. 2013, 2014, 2015); programs and services are more accessible for geographically isolated families (Becher et al. 2015); suitable for both high (Bollen et al. 2014; Tait 2013) and low (Tait 2013) conflicts; a more formal tone may be adopted, leading to enhanced focus on the issue as opposed to the emotion (Gramatikov and Klaming 2012); convenience, flexibility, and cost-effectiveness (Schramm and McCaulley 2012); time-efficiency, netrocracy, and minimisation of aggravating or distracting non-verbal cues (Brennan 2011); enhances parent self-determination and increases family privacy (González Martín 2015); maintains a record of communication and written expression may be more suitable for some people than verbal expression (Knight and Hunter 2013); safety (Rossi et al. 2017); and environmental benefits, document sharing, ability to observe self on videoconferencing platforms which can assist one in adjusting their reactions or behaviour, accommodation of time-zone differences, and reduction of conflicts of interests and privacy concerns within small communities (Tait 2013). Asynchronous communication is a unique component of ODR systems, with additional advantages including the ability for delayed communication to allow time for reflection, considered responses, moderated emotions, and active listening or reading (Bollen et al. 2014; Lavi 2014).

Brennan (2011) also argues that ODR can facilitate 'therapeutic jurisprudence', that is, the potential for law procedures to promote wellbeing. As family disputes are high in conflict and unhelpful emotions, the transformation of the legal system to provide more therapeutic benefit is an idea deserving of more research. Brennan suggests that one way to increase therapeutic jurisprudence is to provide spaces for parent empowerment and self-determination in a process that has largely been court-driven. However, Knight and Hunter's (2013) review on the *Raising Children Network*, an educational, informative, and evidence-based website for parents in Australia, is the only ODR service and reference in the literature that encouraged parental autonomy by actively collaborating with parents to develop service content.

Disadvantages of OFDR Challenges unique to online platforms as compared to face-to-face methods include: limited awareness of ODR systems for both professionals and the public (Araszkiewicz et al. 2013, 2014, 2015; Knight and Hunter 2013); potential for dishonesty (Augar and Zeleznikow 2014); concerns about confidentiality of information (Bollen et al. 2014); lack of room for emotional expressivity (Gramatikov and Klaming 2012); disengagement from the process, information 'thin', and less therapeutic (Brennan 2011); disempowering due to low computer literacy or no accommodations for cultural differences or hearing or visually impaired individuals (González Martín 2015); can take a while to incorporate technology into services, poor quality technology in disadvantaged or geographically isolated areas, difficulty in verifying the qualifications of the mediator, and security concerns (Knight and Hunter 2013); frustration from delayed responses and technology fatigue (Jani 2012); rapport may take a while to develop and communication may be misinterpreted (Lavi 2014); technical failures and inequality if one partner is more proficient with technology (Tait 2013).

Some of the research, however, presents solutions to assist in overcoming some of these challenges. Regarding frustrations resulting from asynchronous communication and the delays in replies, Jani (2012) proposes that mediators develop and enforce guidelines that are agreed upon by all parties. These rules for how parties should conduct themselves during the mediation process are referred to as an 'Agreement to Mediate' in MediateBC's *Distance Mediation Project*, an agreement that all parties must sign prior to the commencement of mediation. Similarly, both Bollen et al. (2014) and Gramatikov and Klaming (2012) outline 48-h deadlines in responding to the other parties' message on their asynchronous online mediation platforms.

To overcome the problem of verifying the credentials of the mediator, Jani (2012) also recommends that the mediator should set up a professional website where their qualifications are listed. Both Bowers et al. (2011) and Augar and Zeleznikow (2014) emphasise the importance of clients having access to valid information, and the responsibility of ODR program developers and mediators in making sure that this information is accessible.

The gap in public consciousness about the existence of ODR services requires resources to be invested into marketing and promotion. Tait (2013) describes how social media was used to promote the *Distance Mediation Project* in Canada, with Twitter and a blog dedicated to OFDR practice being reported as the most successful tools for engagement. She also recommends that the choice of media platform should be guided by the intended target audience for the ODR service. In their review on Relationship Australia Victoria's internet presence, Augar and Zeleznikow (2014) detail the organisation's commitment to employing staff who monitor and maintain the organisation's website, Twitter, and Facebook page.

Technology Some authors (e.g., González Martín 2015; Lavi 2014; Tait 2013) point out that using technology in mediation does not just refer to the tools that assist in the actual mediation process. It can also refer to the methods by which clients search the internet to locate a mediator, how mediators advertise their services, how clients research laws relating to their issues as well as learning about the mediation process. Additionally, Tait (2013) recommends that mediators consider using several different types of technology within the one case. The mediators interviewed in her evaluation typically reported using telephones for initial contact and screening, videoconferencing for pre-mediation sessions, either telephones or videoconferencing for mediation, and email for any post-mediation communication. However, Tait further recommends that the selection of technology should be appropriate for the case (e.g., text communication methods for high-conflict couples), that every party has access to the same technology, and that the technology can offer a sufficient level of confidentiality. MediateBC's *Distance Mediation Guidelines* (2nd Edition) also implore the mediator to consider the security, limitations, capabilities, costs, complexity, and reliability of the technology (Jani 2012).

Despite the encouraging reflections of the authors on the benefits of ODR and the quickly advancing nature of technology, several authors (e.g., Augar and Zeleznikow 2014; González Martín 2015; Jani 2012; Knight and Hunter 2013) argue that online systems should only be used to complement face-to-face services rather than substitute for them entirely. To illustrate, LaMarca (2012) describes how some US states have granted virtual visitation rights to noncustodial parents; however it is often the case that courts rule for this type of visitation not to replace face-to-face contact.

Similarly, Lavi (2014) argues that the unique technologies available to a mediator in ODR platforms should be used in innovative ways, rather than simply transferring face-to-face mediation to online forms. Bowers et al. (2011) found in their review of six online divorce education programs that all appeared to have been moved online without consideration of the original prospects available with technology. One of their recommendations was to take advantage of the technology to facilitate connection among parents taking the course via the use of a discussion board. This recommendation is echoed by Schramm and McCaulley (2012) in their evaluation of the *Focus on Kids* divorce education program.

Bellucci and Zeleznikow (2006) introduce the Family Winner system[1] to support mediators to suggest trade-offs to their clients. Such software has the potential to provide support in preparing parenting plans. Our Family Wizard[2] (Barsky 2016) is used by both US separated parents and courts to ensure cordial conversations between parents.

Processes Pearlstein et al. (2012) assigned ODR processes to three categories: negotiation (without third party intervention), mediation (with third party intervention, but outcomes are non-binding), and arbitration (with third party intervention, which can be binding). While hybrid processes exist, this section will focus on the individualized and independent aspects. There are arguments that some processes perform better for certain conflicts over others, for example Goltsman et al. (2009) demonstrated that mediation is preferred to negotiation when conflict is intermediate while the opposite holds true for when the conflict is low.

Each process has advantages and disadvantages that disputing parties should consider prior to engagement with a particular service. These factors should also be considered in light of how the process changes with the introduction of the 'fourth party', the ODR system. Sela (2018) argued that 'process' consists of both method

[1]See https://www.youtube.com/watch?v=YOZczuvrou4 last viewed 22 February 2019.

[2]See https://www.ourfamilywizard.com last viewed 22 February 2019.

(e.g., negotiation, mediation, or arbitration) *and* the technology used (e.g., automated or human-controlled). She posited that this interaction has implications for how procedural justice is perceived, that is, the fairness of the procedure in dispute resolution. In an experiment with university students using the ODR system *EZSettle*, Sela found that human arbitrators and automated mediators were perceived to deliver more procedural justice than their automated arbitrator and human mediator counterparts, respectively. In each preferred setting, participants reported feeling that they had more agency in the process and that their voices were heard and valued by the automated or human third party.

In the current literature review, the processes located tended to focus on virtual mediation (Bollen et al. 2014; Gramatikov and Klaming 2012; Knight and Hunter 2013 "RAQ's OFDR project"; Tait 2013; Thomson 2011). Both Bollen et al. (2014) and Gramatikov and Klaming (2012) assessed the extent to which the participants of their programs perceived distributive, procedural, interpersonal, and informational justice to have occurred. Additional similarities across the two studies include that both were conducted in the Netherlands and both relied on asynchronous forms of communication. However, Bollen and colleagues were most interested in comparing the experiences of male and female parents in terms of perceptions of justice while Gramatikov and Klaming conducted a more general, overarching evaluation of the program. Results found that both programs received high ratings across all four types of justice although Bollen et al. reported that women perceived the program as facilitating more procedural and interpersonal justice than did men. Gramatikov and Klaming, on the other hand, found a non-significant difference between men and women for both of these types of justice, although men did rate procedural justice higher. In addition, Gramatikov and Klaming found that men reported spending more on out-of-pocket costs during the mediation process than women, while women reported higher levels of frustration and anger than men. Summarising their findings, Bollen et al. suggest that OFDR can be an empowering platform for women, while Gramatikov and Klaming argue that women may be disadvantaged and distressed by OFDR systems, at least when relying on asynchronous means of communication. As such, ensuring access to justice has important implications for dispute system design.

Ebner and Zeleznikow (2015) claim that for ODR systems to be acceptable to users, they must address issues of fairness, trust and security. Zeleznikow and Bellucci (2012) have developed a set of important factors that should be incorporated into "fair" negotiation support processes and tools. These factors include: Transparency Highlighting and clarifying the shadow of the law and Limited discovery.

Netocracy Online mediation and dispute resolution services are commended for their ability to foster equality between parties and 'levelling the playing field'. Specifically, technology is suggested to increase justice and fairness in FDR processes and outcomes due to the removal of physicality and the added feeling of safety (particularly relevant in physically abusive domestic violence situations), the objective of achieving win-win solutions, and the potential for overcoming mediator biases that may inadvertently favour one party over the other (i.e., the 'halo-effect'; Brennan 2011).

A recognition of the potential for power imbalances in mediation is not novel. In her seminal article "*The Mediation Alternative: Process Dangers for Women*", Grillo (1991) identifies how women can be disempowered in relation to their husbands within the divorce mediation process. Specifically, she argues that, within a heteronormative framework, women tend to adopt a relational sense of self, which emphasizes co-operation and an avoidance of conflict, which can be manipulated by, and in favour of, a more individualized and assertive identity (read: masculine-oriented). Brennan (2011) also suggests that inequalities occur when one party feels guilt for the relationship ending and, consequently, accepts unfair settlements in an attempt to alleviate that guilt.

Instances of domestic violence further complicate the balancing of the power scales between parties. Hughes (1995) outlines five types of power that occur and interact within domestic violence cases, all of which may be used by a perpetrator during mediation: economic, intellectual, physical, emotional, and procedural power. The author, among others (e.g., Dunnigan 2003; Field 1998; Hughes 1995), questions the ability of the FDR mediator to effectively identify and manage these abuses of power due to the skillful deception of the perpetrator in concealing patterns of violence or the unawareness of the victim that they are being victimised.

Concerning the consideration of power imbalances in the online domain of family law, Barsky (2016) cautions that a mediator needs to avoid the assumption that online processes are inherently fairer just because of 'thin' information or geographical distance. He further argues that mediators should assess for power imbalances in OFDR platforms by examining whether both parties are equally proficient in using the technology, whether they can both easily afford the technology, and whether they are both comfortable expressing themselves in the selected mode of communication. Calls for more thorough and ongoing assessments of domestic violence in offline FDR can be echoed in OFDR as well, with mediators and intake workers undertaking professional training to identify subtle indicators that one or more of the five types of power is being enacted within the mediation environment, regardless of the medium (Dunnigan 2003; Field 1998).

Ethical Considerations Barsky (2016) leads a discussion on the ethics to be considered when engaging in online systems for FDR. He outlines that mediators must be cognisant of ethical challenges unique to OFDR systems, such as ensuring that an app is valid and appropriate prior to referring it to, or using it with, a client (i.e., duty of care), being able to critically evaluate one's competencies in using a specific technology, ensuring that clients are properly informed about a technology before they make a decision whether or not to use it (i.e., informed consent), ensuring technology is secure and private, and developing boundaries between professional and personal use of technology. Furthermore, Augar and Zeleznikow (2014) emphasise the need to protect confidentiality within online platforms, particularly regarding the potential for parties to record sessions. Rules surrounding appropriate behaviour (i.e., 'netiquette'; Augar and Zeleznikow) may be part of an Agreement to Mediate (Jani 2012).

All these considerations and more have been carefully reflected in recent developments of guidelines and standards in the ODR field. Namely, Wing (2016) in collaboration with the National Center for Technology and Dispute Resolution (NCTDR), presented The Ethical Principles for Online Dispute Resolution (herein, 'Principles') as a values-driven guide to best practice. Seventeen principles were offered with overlapping content with existing dispute resolution standards (such as confidentiality, impartiality, and competence) as well as unique online-specific considerations (such as security and integration). Although not intended to be prescriptive, the Principles provide the foundation for which current and future online-enhanced dispute resolution services may be designed, implemented, and evaluated. The Principles are interdependent and to be flexibly applied with regard to contextual and cultural differences. Building on these principles, the International Council for Online Dispute Resolution (ICODR) has recently compiled a set of nine standards to be applied broadly across ODR programs.[3]

Exon (2017) also draws attention to the potential expansion of The Model Standards of Conduct for Mediators in order to be more inclusive of online dispute resolution practice. She recommends that the existing nine Standards be complemented with a tenth Standard specific to the issues apparent in ODR, such as fourth-parties and programmers, while also amending the original nine Standards to include a consideration of how technology changes the way mediators practice. Contrasting this 'evolutionary' approach, Exon also proposes a 'revolutionary' approach whereby an entirely new set of Standards are developed to reflect the unique challenges apparent in ODR services. Relatedly, the International Mediation Institute has focused on these changes to mediator proficiencies within online platforms and have subsequently developed competency criteria.[4]

Rainey (2017) cautions that one set of standards may not be comprehensive enough to cover the diverse needs and responsibilities of different stakeholders and parties within ODR practice. Further, he posits that the current flourishing interest in ODR and its ethical underpinnings has led to the simultaneous and potentially conflicting development of numerous standards. He concludes his concerns by stating that the challenge will be to create a set of standards that are coherent, cohesive, and flexible enough to be widely applicable.

In addition, Lavi (2014) argues for regulation rules in the form of a professional body that would supervise websites that offer OFDR services. She recommends that such processes might include an indicator of quality presented to validated organisations on the basis of pre-post evaluation questionnaires assigned to participating parties. Organisations could also regularly submit data (e.g., percentage of cases

[3]See https://icodr.org/standards/ last accessed 11 May 2020.

[4]See https://www.imimediation.org/about/who-are-imi/odr-tf/ last accessed 12 May 2020.

ending in agreement, average duration for cases) to the regulatory body as a form of governance and accountability.

Schmitz and Wing (2020) consider Beneficial and Ethical ODR for Family Issues. They argue that The International Center for Online Dispute Resolution (ICODR) has ODR Standards[5] which require that ethical ODR systems must be:

Accessible ODR must be easy for parties to find and participate in and not limit their right to representation. ODR should be available through both mobile and desktop channels, minimize costs to participants, and be easily accessed by people with different physical ability levels

Accountable ODR systems must be continuously accountable to the institutions, legal frameworks, and communities that they serve.

Competent ODR providers must have the relevant expertise in dispute resolution, legal, technical execution, language, and culture required to deliver competent, effective services in their target areas. ODR services must be timely and use participant time efficiently.

Confidential ODR must maintain the confidentiality of party communications in line with policies that must be made public around (a) who will see what data, and (b) how that data can be used.

Equal ODR must treat all participants with respect and dignity.

Fair/Impartial/Neutral ODR must treat all parties equally and in line with due process, without bias or benefits for or against individuals, groups, or entities. Conflicts of interest of providers, participants, and system administrators must be disclosed in advance of commencement of ODR services.

Legal ODR must abide by and uphold the laws in all relevant jurisdictions.

Secure ODR providers must ensure that data collected and communications between those engaged in ODR is not shared with any unauthorized parties. Users must be informed of any breaches in a timely manner.

Transparent ODR providers must explicitly disclose in advance (a) the form and enforceability of dispute resolution processes and outcomes, and (b) the risks and benefits of participation. Data in ODR must be gathered, managed, and presented in ways to ensure it is not misrepresented or out of context.

Ebner and Zeleznikow (2016) also consider the governance of ODR. They argue that the ODR environment is similar to the 'Wild West'. Unless there is appropriate governance of ODR, users may have very little trust in the processes and hence be reluctant to engage with them.

ODR generally knows little or no regulation, authority, standards, or monitoring. Within the field itself, governance is virtually non-existent: no body monitors quality

[5]http://icodr.org/index.php/standards/ Last viewed July 30 2020.

control, no well-recognized and accepted standards of practice exist, no-one deals with complaints or investigates bad practices. Because ODR practice is by nature Internet-based, any external supervision, such as that stemming from consumer protection laws, is weak, and subject to jurisdictional shortcomings.

Most of the early ODR providers, and many of the current ones, have chosen the organizational/commercial model of "*service provider company.*" In this model, the management team behind the company is not personally identified (or even named at all). Many, perhaps most, service providers do not relate substantively to the identity, qualifications, or training of their neutrals. They do not share their code of practice, even if they have one; they do not share whether they subscribe to codes of practice formulated by organizations in other fields.

Ebner and Zeleznikow (2016) claim there are four potential governance models:

1. *A no-governance model:* This model would recognize ODR as a free-market activity, and not one that any central body of practitioners chooses to regulate. In this model, actor's norms would be regulated by externally imposed laws; the less external regulation, or the weaker its enforcement, the stronger would be the impact of market forces on actors' activity.
2. *A self-governance model:* This model would recognize that normative, ethical behavior is preferable for all, but would choose not to engage with or monitor individual actors' activities in this regard. A central voluntary entity would recommend best practices, ethical standards, or competency baselines and invite anybody identifying with the field to conform to them. Such compliance would be completely voluntary, with the recommended norms having no binding force, and without a monitoring body or enforcement measures. Compliance would be subjectively self-enforced—each member entity would determine whether it was complying with the standards.
3. *An internal governance model:* by industry groups. This model would create structures and organizations to set practice standards, create accreditation schemes, conduct monitoring of practitioners, and enforce compliance. This could follow a guild or association model in which elected representatives interact with external stakeholders to advance policies seen as beneficial to the field, to limit the activity of actors unidentified with the organized field, and to advance the field's status to that of an independent profession. Whilst there are professional bodies in Australia that could offer governance in IT (such as the Australian Computer Society[6]) and ADR (the Resolution Institute[7]) there is no appropriate body for ODR either in Australia or globally.
4. *An external governance model*: should and would the courts or governments regulate ODR? This model would recognize that the field is best organized from the outside. Individual actors in the field could provide expertise to external bodies directly or indirectly regulating ODR activity, and the field as a whole

[6]https://www.acs.org.au/ last viewed 30 July 2020.

[7]https://www.resolution.institute/about-us last viewed 30 July 2020.

could seek greater external engagement that could increase ODR's adoption and institutionalization across a wide range of industries, jurisdictions, and contexts. Under this model, the field would not seek to create internal structures, promote standards, or create qualifications, independent of these external contexts.

These models are proposed as a platform from which to initiate further discussion around the future of governance in ODR. To be accepted by users, ODR providers must subscribe to a rigorous governance model.

Mediator Competencies and Needs The literature shows that online mediation is a complex process that can easily overwhelm inexperienced or inadequately supported mediators. MediateBC's *Practice Guidelines*, developed from the *Distance Family Mediation Project*, is an important resource for mediators, as it comprehensively outlines all aspects of the OFDR process that a mediator should consider prior to commencing with the technology (Jani 2012). They emphasise the need for mediators to carefully consider the technology they are using and acknowledge how the addition of technology fundamentally changes the mediation process. The Guidelines recommend techniques to:

- overcome the minimisation of non-verbal cues (e.g., asking questions, checking in regularly);
- assess if a case is suitable for online intervention; engage in risk management procedures; and screen for domestic violence. An appendix also includes a checklist for mediators to use in order to assess and monitor their on-screen presence for videoconferencing technologies (e.g., lighting, background, clothing, position, and personal presentation).

Unique mediator skills required on online platforms include: managing multiple online meeting rooms (i.e., private and joint rooms), assisting parties in using technology, and building rapport and trust online (Lavi 2014); translating mediation skills to the online environment and technological proficiency (González Martín 2015); managing distractions, technical difficulties, and silences (Thomson 2011); being aware of the different laws governing each state or country (LaMarca 2012); staying on top of advances in technology (Barsky 2016; Jani 2012); and being aware of the different resources and referral agencies available in each state or country (Jani 2012). Tait (2013) notes that the move to online mediation can result in a high cognitive load during the learning stages, and consequently emphasises that a professional *must* first have robust skills in mediation prior to moving to online platforms.

Interviews with mediators for the *Distance Mediation Project Phase III* evaluation (Tait 2013) showed that there was a need to support professionals both in technical aspects of systems (via a technical support team) and in using mediation on these systems (via a peer support group). There is also a need to ensure that professionals are ready to engage with technology.

In their research on Relationships Australia Queensland staff preparing to develop and adopt an OFDR system (within the context of the larger research and evaluation study described in Chap. 4 of this book), Casey and Wilson-Evered (2012) recommended that organisations offer staff training, assess staff readiness, and target any distrust in the technology prior to implementation of the tools. To this end, the authors extended Venkatesh et al. (2003) unified theory of acceptance and use of technology (UTAUT) model to include trust toward the system and personal web innovativeness (that is, exploratory behavior with technology). They then tested the modified model with 127 RAQ staff prior to engagement with the OFDR pilot program to elucidate the relationship between attitudes and behavior intention to adopt the system. Staff reported positive attitudes towards the use of OFDR, as well as high perceptions of OFDR usefulness and trustworthiness. Regarding testing of the model, Casey and Wilson-Evered found that performance expectancy (the belief that the system will contribute to positive outcomes), effort expectancy (perceived ease of use), and trust in technology were related to intentions to adopt the system and therefore should be targeted in staff training and preparation for the implementation of new system. As such, these findings have implications for the necessity of pre-contemplation staff assessments in order to maximise organizational uptake of new technology, although the extended model is also proposed to have utility for client readiness assessments.

Client Characteristics Of the seven empirical studies, the average age of participants was approximately 38 years old, women were more likely to be involved (56%), almost all individuals were in heterosexual relationships (Gramatikov and Klaming 2012 reported that there may have been two same-sex couples in their sample), and the vast majority of participants were white (91%). However, these data are partial as the quality of information collected and reported among studies was variable. Knight and Hunter (2013) reported that young people are more likely to engage in online services, although Tait (2013) reported a higher participation rate in the *Distance Mediation Project* from individuals 30 to 39 years of age. The *Project* also found that older age groups (i.e., 40–49 years) were more likely to use telephone services than videoconferencing and that telephone services were under-utilised by clients earning higher incomes.

In their research comparing online and face-to-face versions of the *Focus on Kids* program, Schramm and McCaulley (2012) noted that far more men were utilising the online system than the face-to-face option. Similarly, Augar and Zeleznikow (2014) posited that men may benefit from online services to assist in adjustment post-divorce, particularly if they lose primary residence of any children. Online counselling and support groups may help to reduce isolation, improve wellbeing, and increase connection with others who have shared experiences. Additionally, in Knight and Hunter's (2013) case study review of the *mymob* app developed by Stepfamilies Australia, they observed that the app was well received by male parents, who indicated that they preferred the anonymity of technology.

There is also minimal discussion in the literature about why clients discontinue or avoid OFDR services. Tait (2013) collected and presented evidence on the reasons why individuals who inquired about the *Distance Mediation Project* did not proceed with their inquiry, with responses indicating that either one or both parties were not interested, or parties preferred face-to-face mediation. Only one respondent indicated that they were not comfortable using technology.[8] Tait does caution for self-selection biases in the data, however, and the sample size was small.

Children There is limited discussion in the OFDR literature about the role of children in child welfare disputes, however in MediateBC's *Distance Mediation Guidelines* (2nd Edition), it is strongly advised that children are not involved during the mediation process (Jani 2012). In fact, parents are instructed to ensure that their children are completely removed from the location in which the online mediation is to take place so that the likelihood of children over-hearing the process is minimised. However, in a passing comment in his discussion paper, González Martín (2015) suggested that technology can be used to engage a child in the mediation process in certain US jurisdictions, depending on the age and maturity of the child. LaMarca (2012) also addressed the role of the child in his work reviewing the literature of 'virtual visitation'. Specifically, he restored the child's autonomy in child welfare arrangements by stating that even though parents and the courts may approve online tools to connect non-resident parents with their children, the children themselves need to express interest in engaging with technology and this process. In Australia, children rarely directly participate in child welfare mediations. Rather their views are sought by and presented by children's representatives. So OFDR is not directly used by children.

3.4 Discussion

The intention of the current literature review was to understand the current research and practice on online family dispute resolution systems within Australian and international contexts. From the 19 records located through a systematic search protocol, it is clear that despite the growing interest in, advancement of, and access to technology there remains a lot to be done in regard to the empirical investigation of the ODR effectiveness as it is applied to family law. The majority of research to date appears to come out of the United States, although Australia is also an identified leader in OFDR platforms.

Of the four Australian-centric sources located in this literature review, it is clear that a varied range of programs are being developed for use in family-related ODR and adjacent services, from readiness assessments (Casey and Wilson-Evered 2012), online counselling (Augar and Zeleznikow 2014; Knight and Hunter 2013), co-parenting tools, and educational resources (Knight and Hunter 2013), as well as OFDR programs themselves (Knight and Hunter 2013; Thomson 2011). As has been outlined in previous chapters, these services are developed within a context that is child-focused and adversarial-avoidant. Making several different services available

[8]Probably because most parents of children involved in parenting disputes are under 50.

allows for consumers to choose the most appropriate option for them depending on their circumstances, needs, and preferences. In this way, Australian OFDR service programmers and designers acknowledge the diversity both within the population and those seeking family dispute-oriented solutions. The next section of this chapter further expands upon the current range of Australian-developed OFDR-and-related services.

Further, Knight and Hunter's (2013) review on the *Raising Children Network*, an educational, informative, and evidence-based website for parents in Australia, is the only OFDR service found in the literature that encouraged parental autonomy by actively collaborating with parents to develop service content, thereby leading the way for empowering service design.

Cross-culturally there appears to be a bias towards communicating the benefits of using technology in FDR processes, although a predominant theme identified was the argument that OFDR should complement, but not replace, existing traditional services. Indeed, Zeleznikow (2017) noted that there is an increasing trend to move from fully automated ODR to approaches where human decision making is supported.

The ability to make any conclusive statements about the utility and impact of online technologies for family dispute resolution is limited, however a number of key themes that may assist in future program development and research can be identified. There is first and foremost a prioritisation of the child(ren)'s wellbeing in any child welfare matters, over and above the particular interests and needs of the separating parents. However, the voices of the children to whom these parenting and legal decisions affect are largely absent from the literature, with mixed opinion as to whether or not they should be involved in mediation processes.

There are a wide range of services available to support separating families throughout their transition, however the appropriateness of different types of online services, or even the decision to use an online platform at all, should be determined on a case by case basis. Not all disputes will be suitable for technological intervention and a number of factors beyond mere convenience need to be carefully considered by the mediator prior to using OFDR platforms. More quality empirical research on existing and developing programs will assist mediators to make informed decisions about which services are likely to be effective for a particular case.

When technology is used, mediators and program developers should take advantage of the unique capabilities that the technology offers, rather than transferring face-to-face practices to the online environment. This new environment also adds original challenges of which a mediator must be cognisant, particularly those challenges relating to privacy and security of information, proficiency of use, and development of trust and rapport, to name a few.

In general, the evidence that is currently available reveals that technologies can enhance FDR practice and contribute to family wellbeing in the midst of a stressful life event. However, potential users of technology should remain appropriately cautious and acknowledge that online programs and services are not without their disadvantages. With adequate training, a respect for the system's limitations, and an appreciation for the needs of different disputing parties, OFDR platforms can help separating families obtain equitable and just outcomes.

Gaps in the Research As aforementioned, there were no randomised controlled trials located during the course of this literature review. Although one article (Rossi et al. 2017) cited a forthcoming study using a RCT design to compare the effectiveness of shuttle and online mediation approaches to family disputes presenting with family violence, the lack of methodologically rigorous research in this field requires amendment. Family law is an area in which parents and children already experience high vulnerability and elevated emotions, so it is critical that services have demonstrated effectiveness and quality in order to be ethical. The seven empirical studies in this review had substantial limitations in collecting, analysing, and reporting their data, including but not limited to: no control or comparison group, small effect sizes reported, reliance on self-report, homogenous participants (i.e., high proportions of white parents reported), small sample sizes, selection biases, low response rates, invalid measures used, no follow-up data collected, and poor description of sampling procedures and subsequent participant attrition. Barsky (2016), Bowers et al. (2011) and Rossi et al. (2017) have all identified the need for more rigorous empirical research in the field of OFDR.

3.5 ODR-Related Services and Programs

3.5.1 Method

A search was also conducted in September 2018 to locate existing and active ODR and online mediation services in Australia and internationally.[9] Conley Tyler and Bretherton (2003) conducted a similar extensive search for existing services, however due to the rapid development of technology since 2003 it was considered pertinent and timely to perform an updated search. Additionally, Conley Tyler and Bretherton conducted a general search of ODR services, noting few that specialized in family-oriented disputes. Later, Conley-Tyler and McPherson (2006) completed a review of services specific to OFDR, however this review was not comprehensive of all services available in the market at the time. As such, this search was conducted with the intention of locating those services catering to OFDR, in addition to ODR. Services were located via open Google searching, blogs dedicated to ODR, Conley Tyler and Bretherton's (2003) paper on ODR, and recommendations from leaders in the field. No comprehensive or separate search was conducted for online divorce mediation services, co-parenting solutions, or e-courts/online juries although some of these services were identified using these search methods.

[9]For a recent a comprehensive list of ODR providers in the U.S, the reader is referred to Schmitz A, Martinez J (2020) at https://papers.ssrn.com/sol3/papers.cfm?abstract_id=3599511 Last accessed 20 May 2020.

3.5.2 Results

A total of 102 services were located, with 67 rejected after preliminary reviews. Reasons for rejection include inaccessible or inactive websites ($n = 41$), no online services offered ($n = 10$), irrelevant ($n = 8$), and duplicates ($n = 3$). Five resources were found to be marginally relevant to ODR including: online training in conflict management (*Brav*), management tools and software for ODR (*CaseloadManager, Conflict Resolution Software*), general information for ODR (*Cyber Arbitration*), and a directory to find online mediators (*OnlineMediators.com*). This process left 35 services for further review: seven were found to be based in Australia (*Family Resolve, Guided Resolution, interMEDIATE, Life Mediation, The Mediation Experts, MODRON, Reboot Resolve*), fourteen in the United States (*Conflicteam, Endispute,*[10] *It's Over Easy, Legal Faceoff, Mediation-On-The-Go, Modria, Matterhorn ODR, OurDivorceAgreement, Peopleclaim, Rapid Rulings, Settle Today, SettlementIQ, UptoParents, Virtual Courthouse*), four in Canada (*Civil Resolution Tribunal, The International Court for Online Conflict Resolution, MediateBC, Smartsettle*), one in the United Kingdom (*Graham* Ross), one with dual bases in the United Kingdom and Australia (*Resolve Disputes Online*), one in Italy (*RisolviOnline*), one in Germany (*judica*), one in Israel (*Agree Online*), and five mobile applications (*2 houses, mymob, ODR 4 Refugees, Otter, Our Family Wizard*).

An updated review was completed in May 2020 which located eight additional services: one in the Netherlands (*Uit Elkaar*), three in the United States (*Wevorce, hellodivorce, Divorceify*), two in Canada (*MyLawBC, Common Sense Divorce*), one in India (*CREK*) one in both the US and Canada (*coParenter*), for a total of 42 services. Three services, *Legal Faceoff, iudica,* and *OurDivorceAgreement* were removed as they no longer active at the time of the updated review, for a final total of 39 services. An overview of each service is provided in Table 3.1.

The quality and quantity of information available online varies for each service, with only half of the websites providing extensive detail about the steps involved in the mediation process for this service ($n = 21$). Only 13 websites also provide a 'Frequently Asked Questions' page to assist potential consumers in understanding their service while 11 elected not to provide estimations of the cost for service use. Pricing varies considerably, with free ($n = 6$), partially free ($n = 3$), per-case pricing ($n = 13$), and payment-plan ($n = 6$) options. Some services ($n = 15$) also employ competitive techniques in the market, by offering free consultations, demos, or 7-day/30-day service trials.

Regarding target population, the majority of services ($n = 31$; e.g., *UptoParents*) are advertised towards people requiring mediated solutions with the remainder of the services ($n = 5$; e.g., *Matterhorn ODR*) aiming to address the needs of professionals and courts or provide services for both types of users ($n = 3$; e.g., *Guided*

[10]There is an Australian company with the same name that has traditional dispute resolution (and not online) as its focus. See http://www.endispute.com.au/our_mission last viewed 22 February 2019.

Table 3.1 Types of ODR and related services available for varying disputes

Services	Function	Dispute type	Web address
2 houses	Collaboration software (app)	Family disputes	https://www.2houses.com/en/
Agree online	Crowd-sourced ODR	Online disputes (Children)	http://www.agree-online.com/#main
CDMC national (MODRON)	Facilitated negotiation	Range of dispute types	https://cdmcnational.com.au/online-dispute-resolution/
Civil resolution tribunal	e-court	Range of dispute types	https://civilresolutionbc.ca/
Common sense divorce	Facilitated negotiation	Family disputes	https://www.commonsensedivorce.ca/
Conflicteam	Negotiation support systems	Range of dispute types	http://conflicteam.com/
coParenter	Collaboration software (app)	Family disputes	https://coparenter.com/
CREK	ODR platform for mediation, negotiation, and arbitration	Range of dispute types	https://crekodr.com
Divorceify	Information system	Family disputes	https://divorceify.com/home
Endispute	Virtual mediation	Range of dispute types	https://www.jamsadr.com/endispute/
Family resolve	Virtual mediation	Family disputes	https://familyresolve.com.au/
Guided resolution	Negotiation support system	Range of dispute types	https://www.guideresolution.com/
Graham Ross	Virtual mediation	Range of dispute types	https://www.mediate.com/author/Graham-Ross/1433
Hello divorce	Document management; information system	Family disputes	https://hellodivorce.com/
ICOCR	e-court	Range of dispute types	https://www.e-court.ca/web2/blue/icocr/index2AAA.php
interMEDIATE	Virtual mediation	Range of dispute types	https://www.intermediate.com.au/service/telephone-online-service/
It's over easy	Document management; negotiation support system	Family disputes	https://www.itsovereasy.com/
Life mediation	Virtual mediation	Range of dispute types	http://lifemediation.com.au/mediation-process/online-mediation/
Matterhorn ODR	Case management	Range of dispute types	https://getmatterhorn.com/
MediateBC	Virtual mediation; information system	Range of dispute types	http://www.mediatebc.com/
Mediation-on-the-go	Virtual mediation	Family disputes	https://www.equitablemediation.com/

(continued)

Table 3.1 (continued)

Services	Function	Dispute type	Web address
Modria	Negotiation support system	Range of dispute types	https://www.tylertech.com/solutions-products/modria
MyLawBC	Virtual Mediation; Document Management	Family disputes	https://mylawbc.com/
Mymob	Collaboration software (app)	Family disputes	http://mymob.org/
ODR 4 refugees	Virtual mediation (app)	Range of dispute types (Refugees)	http://www.odreurope.com/odr4refugees
Otter	Virtual Mediation (app)	Range of dispute types (Children)	http://www.otterkids.com/
Our family wizard	Collaboration software (app)	Family disputes	https://www.ourfamilywizard.com/
Peopleclaim	Crowd-sourced ODR	Range of dispute types	https://www.peopleclaim.com/
Rapid rulings	Facilitated negotiation	Range of dispute types	https://www.rapidrulings.com/
Reboot resolve	Virtual mediation	Family disputes	https://rebootresolve.com.au/
Resolve disputes online	Case management	Range of dispute types	https://resolvedisputes.online/index.html
Risolvi online	Virtual mediation	E-commerce disputes	https://www.risolvionline.com/index.php?lng_id=14
Settle today	Facilitated negotiation	Range of dispute types	https://settletoday.com/
SettlementIQ	Negotiation support system	Range of dispute types	https://www.settlementiq.com/
Smartsettle	Negotiation support system	Family disputes	https://smartsettle.com
Uit elkaar	Facilitated negotiation	Family disputes	https://uitelkaar.nl/
Uptoparents	Facilitated negotiation, information system	Family disputes	https://www.uptoparents.org/default.aspx
Virtual courthouse	e-court	Range of dispute types	http://www.virtualcourthouse.com/
Wevorce	Facilitated negotiation	Family disputes	https://www.wevorce.com/

Resolution). For those requiring mediation, services are either self-directed online platforms ($n = 14$; e.g., *2houses*), mediator or third-party intervening platforms ($n = 14$; e.g., *Endispute*), or a combination of both ($n = 6$, e.g., *Settle Today*). As such, the services vary in their approaches to dispute resolution, including virtual mediation ($n = 12$), facilitated negotiation ($n = 7$), negotiation support systems ($n = 6$), collaboration software ($n = 4$), information systems ($n = 4$), e-courts ($n = 3$), document management ($n = 3$), case management ($n = 2$), and crowd-sourced ODR ($n = 2$). The total of services exceeds 39 as several services provided multiple functions.

The majority of the services ($n = 22$) provide support for a range of disputes (i.e., tenant, commercial, family, workplace, and general disputes), while a substantial minority ($n = 15$) focus solely on family-related issues, and only a few ($n = 2$) target online-originating disputes. However, it should be noted that these results are unlikely to be an accurate reflection of the proportion of services targeting family disputes in comparison to other dispute types due to the biased search focus on OFDR.

As an identified benefit of OFDR over court-based approaches is the efficiency of the service, it would be expected that potential consumers would be interested in knowing up-front how long they would expect for their dispute to be resolved. Relying solely on the information available on the service websites (as opposed to independent evaluations), only 12 services provided an estimation from commencement to completion, ranging from 20 min (for everyday disputes in *coParenter*) to a year (until Divorce Decree is awarded with *Common Sense Divorce*).

Exclusive use of videoconferencing software and telephone communication is rare ($n = 2$; e.g., *Family Resolve*), with most services ($n = 16$; e.g., *Otter*) opting for text communication methods (i.e., email, chat messaging), a combination of all three approaches ($n = 13$; e.g., *ODR 4 Refugees*), or a combination of technological and face-to-face mediation options ($n = 5$; e.g., *interMEDIATE*). It is perhaps a surprising finding that so few services utilize 'rich' forms of communication (i.e., both auditory and visual information) and instead predominantly rely on text-based communication. Pearlstein et al. (2012) also found that videoconferencing tools were under-utilised in their review of North American ODR services. This finding may reflect the early and continued development of videoconferencing abilities in OFDR and general ODR platforms, or it could reflect a consumer preference for written forms of communication, the benefits of which have already been described in the previous review.

Araszkiewicz et al. (2013, 2014, 2015) and Knight and Hunter (2013) argued that ODR services need to be better promoted in the public consciousness; this review has demonstrated that such promotion might be better served by having more detailed and up-to-date service information available to consumers. The information in this review was difficult to locate through publicly-accessible means which may hinder engagement with online services, particularly since one of the expected benefits of ODR services is the ease with which it is used. It may be recommended that future research assesses what information the potential users of these services require in their decision-making processes and how they locate such information in order to better understand why consumers choose ODR over alternative options, and how they choose between different ODR options. Since Conley Tyler and Bretherton's (2003) review, it is clear that the number of ODR services available for family disputes has increased across time, thereby reflecting the market growth required to meet public need. It is expected that more OFDR options across the globe will being to enter the market as either an adjunct to previously existing services or as a stand-alone, exclusively online service.

References

Araszkiewicz M, Łopatkiewicz A, Zienkiewicz A (2013) Parent Plan Support System - context, functions and knowledge base. Paper presented at the international conference on business information systems Heidelberg, Berlin, Springer, 19–20 June, pp 160–171

Araszkiewicz M, Łopatkiewicz A, Zienkiewicz A (2014) The role of new information technologies in alternative resolution of divorce disputes. Eur Sci J 1:549–558

Araszkiewicz M, Łopatkiewicz A, Zienkiewicz A, Zurek T (2015) Representation of an actual divorce dispute in the parenting plan support system. Paper presented at The 15th international conference on artificial intelligence and Law San Diego, CA, 8–12 June, pp 166–170

Augar N, Zeleznikow J (2014) Developing online support and counseling to enhance family dispute resolution in Australia. Group Decis Negot 23:515–532

Barsky AE (2016) The ethics of app-assisted family mediation. Conflict Resol Q 34:31–42

Becher E, Cronin S, McCann E, Olson KA, Powell S, Marczak MS (2015) Parents forever: evaluation of an online divorce education program. J Divorce Remarriage 56:261–276

Bellucci E, Zeleznikow J (2006) Developing negotiation decision support systems that support mediators: a case study of the Family_Winner system. J Artificial Intell Law 13:233–271

Bollen KNL, Verbeke A, Euwema MC (2014) Computers work for women: gender differences in e-supported divorce mediation. Comp Hum Behav 30:230–237

Bowers JR, Mitchell ET, Hardesty JL, Hughes R Jr (2011) A review of online divorce education programs. Family Court Rev 49:776–787

Brennan R (2011) Mismatch.com: online dispute resolution and divorce. Cardozo J Conflict Resol 13:197–224

Casey T, Wilson-Evered E (2012) Predicting uptake of technology innovations in online family dispute resolution services: an application and extension of the UTAUT. Comp Hum Behav 28:2034–2045

Conley Tyler M, Bretherton D (2003) Developing an online mediation culture: the fourth generation of online ADR. Paper presented at the 2nd Asia Pacific Mediation Forum, Singapore, pp 1–19

Conley-Tyler MH, McPherson MW (2006) Online dispute resolution and family disputes. J Family Stud 12:165–183

Cronin S, Becher EH, McCann E, McGuire J, Powell S (2017) Relational conflict and outcomes from an online divorce education program. Evaluation Program Plan 62:49–55

Dunnigan A (2003) Restoring power to the powerless: the need to reform California's mandatory mediation for victims of domestic violence. Univ San Francisco Law Rev 37:1031–1064

Ebner N, Zeleznikow J (2015) Fairness, trust and security in online dispute resolution. Hamline Univ School Law J Public Law Policy 36:vi. https://digitalcommons.hamline.edu/jplp/vol36/iss2/6

Ebner N, Zeleznikow J (2016) No sheriff in town: governance for the ODR field. Negot J 32:297–323

Exon SN (2017) Ethics and online dispute resolution: from evolution to revolution. Ohio St J Disp Resol 32:665–664

Field R (1998) Mediation and the art of power (im)balancing. Queensland Univ Technol Law J 12:264–273

Goltsman M, Hörner J, Pavlov G, Squintani F (2009) Mediation, arbitration, and negotiation. J Econ Theory 144:1397–1420

González Martín N (2015) International parental child abduction and mediation. Anuario Mexicano de Derecho Internacional 15:353–412

Gramatikov M, Klaming L (2012) Getting divorced online: procedural and outcome justice in online divorce mediation. J Law Family Stud 14:97–120

Grillo T (1991) The mediation alternative: process dangers for women. Yale Law J 100:1545–1610

Hughes SH (1995) Elizabeth's story: exploring power imbalances in divorce mediation. Geo J Legal Ethics 8:553–596

Jani S (2012) Mediating from a distance: suggested practice guidelines for family mediators, 2nd edn. MediateBC, Vancouver

Knight K, Hunter C (2013) Using technology in service delivery to families, children and young people, no. 17, Child Family Community Australia (CFCA). https://aifs.gov.au/cfca/publications/using-technology-service-delivery-families-children

LaMarca J (2012) Virtually possible - using the internet to facilitate custody and parenting beyond relocation. Rutgers Comp Technol Law J 38:146–172

Lavi D (2014) No more click-click in here: e-mediation in divorce disputes-the reality and the desirable. Cardozo J Conflict Resol 16:479–541

Lodder A, Zeleznikow J (2005) Developing an online dispute resolution environment: dialogue tools and negotiation systems in a three step model. Harv Negot Law Rev 10:287–338

Lodder A, Zeleznikow J (2010) Enhanced dispute resolution through the use of information technology. Cambridge University Press, Cambridge

Pearlstein A, Hanson B, Ebner N (2012) ODR in North America. In: Abdel Wahab MS, Katsh E, Rainey D (eds) Online dispute resolution: theory and practice. Eleven International Publishing, The Hague, pp 431–452

Rainey D (2017) Creating standards for ODR. Int J Online Disp Resol 4:21–25

Rossi FS, Holtzworth-Munroe A, Applegate AG, Beck CJ, Adams JM, Hale DF (2017) Shuttle and online mediation: a review of available re-search and implications for separating couples reporting intimate partner violence or abuse. Family Court Rev 55:390–403

Schmitz AJ, Wing L (2020) Beneficial and ethical ODR for family issues. Family Court Review (forthcoming)

Schramm DG, McCaulley G (2012) Divorce education for parents: a comparison of online and in-person delivery methods. J Divorce Remarriage 53:602–617

Sela A (2018) Can computers be fair? How automated and human-powered online dispute resolution affect procedural justice in mediation and arbitration. Ohio State J Disp Resol 33:91–148

Tait C (2013) Evaluation of the Distance Family Mediation Project: report on Phase III of the technology-assisted family mediation project. MediateBC, Vancouver, http://www.mediatebc.com/about-mediation/mediating-at-a-distance.aspx

Thomson M (2011) Alternative modes of delivery for family dispute resolution: the telephone dispute resolution service and the online FDR project. J Family Stud 17:253–257

Venkatesh V, Morris M, Davis G, Davis F (2003) User acceptance of information technology: towards a unified view. MIS Q 27:425–478

Wing L (2016) Ethical principles for online dispute resolution: a GPS device for the field. Int J Online Disp Resol 3:12–29

Zeleznikow J (2011) Methods for incorporating fairness into development of an online family dispute resolution environment. Aust Disp Resol J 22:16–21

Zeleznikow J (2014) Comparing the Israel – Palestinian dispute to Australian family mediation. Group Decis Negot J 23:1301–1317

Zeleznikow J (2017) Can artificial intelligence and online dispute resolution enhance efficiency and effectiveness in courts. IJCA 8:30

Zeleznikow J, Bellucci E (2012) Legal fairness in alternative dispute resolution processes – implications for research and teaching. Aust Disp Resol J 23:265–273

Chapter 4
Case Study: The Development and Evaluation of Relationship Australia Queensland's Online Family Dispute Resolution System

Abstract The previous chapter emphasised the need for more methodologically rigorous evidence in online family dispute resolution (OFDR) if these technologically-enhanced services are to be useful and enduring. The contribution of Australia to furthering OFDR knowledge and practice worldwide is exemplified by an innovative pilot project conducted by Relationships Australia Queensland in 2009. Both the development of the software and its subsequent evaluation were evidence-based and intended to adhere to best practice through the adoption of an iterative design that incorporated ongoing quantitative and qualitative data from all stakeholders to optimise system functioning and utility. This chapter summarises processes, findings, and recommendations of this pilot across the four stages of the program design: registration, intake, pre-FDR education, and OFDR. Clients and staff reported largely positive attitudes towards OFDR, with need to appreciate the learning curve involved in navigating the system and how the technology qualitatively changes the mediation process. This pilot sets the standard for the development and evaluation of OFDR services in Australia and worldwide by subjecting the service to extensive systematic testing and evaluation to promote continuous learning and improvement.

4.1 Introduction

In 2009, the Commonwealth Attorney General's Department allocated funds to Relationships Queensland Australia (RAQ) in order to develop and evaluate online family dispute resolution (OFDR) capabilities. The first of its kind in Australia, the process was a laborious and multidisciplinary effort that required the expertise from research, technology, practice, and finance teams.

The figures and the text in this chapter have been reprinted from "Online Family Dispute Resolution Report: Research Evaluation Summary (2011)" by Relationships Australian QLD 2011. Reprinted with permission from Relationships Australia QLD.

E. Wilson-Evered, J. Zeleznikow, *Online Family Dispute Resolution*, Law, Governance and Technology Series 45,
https://doi.org/10.1007/978-3-030-64645-5_4

A provider of a range of relationship services and support, RAQ already offered alternative flexible options for separating parents requiring mediation. Since July 2007, the Telephone Dispute Resolution Service (TDRS) has been funded by the Australia Government to provide nationwide family mediation services concerning parenting and property disputes (Thomson 2011). The TDRS is operated by RAQ in partnership with Relationships Australia New South Wales and operates as a component of the Family Relationship Advice Line (FRAL). The service is equipped to manage requests for interpreters and hearing or speech impairment supports.

The aim of the OFDR project was to increase access to family dispute resolution services, with accessibility to traditional face-to-face services impeded by the rural and remote nature that comprises much of Australian landmass. These barriers to access are disproportionately borne by Aboriginal and Torres Strait Islander communities which exacerbates continued oppression. As part of the OFDR project, a study was conducted to investigate cultural consideration in the design and implementation of the proposed OFDR system so that it would be culturally responsive and appropriate for Aboriginal and Torres Strait Islander peoples. Chapter 5 details the processes and outcomes of these efforts.

Although the existing telephone service bridges some of this gap to access, the advancing nature of technology yields an exciting opportunity to increase the number of options available for family mediation services. The TDRS was thereby identified as an ideal site by the Attorney General to explore the use of extended technologies to provide Family Dispute Resolution services online. The resulting alliance between government and the Not-for-Profit sector presents exciting opportunities for both the general public (in terms of broadening access to Family Dispute Resolution mechanisms) and the Australian mediation community. The opportunity to trial OFDR methods on a national scale represents a unique chance to strengthen empirical knowledge regarding online negotiation and develop best practice guidelines for Internet-based service delivery.

This chapter is a condensed version of a comprehensive evaluation report completed in March 2011 which analysed the effectiveness of a pilot of the OFDR system (Relationships Australia 2011). The reader is encouraged to refer to this document for additional material that space here does not permit. In this chapter, an overview of the process in designing the OFDR platform will first be presented, with due attention paid to technological development, security considerations, and robust testing procedures. The remainder of the chapter will detail the assessment of the system with a systematic examination of each stage of the evaluation process. The chapter will conclude with an overview of recommendations for future practice and research.

4.2 Developing OFDR Capabilities

In the development and evaluation of this innovative system, the following definition of OFDR capabilities was adopted:

> the reliable and effective delivery of OFDR services (i.e. registration, Intake, pre-FDR education, OFDR sessions, client information and referrals) utilising user-appropriate and accessible online technologies (i.e. video conferencing, video streaming, Voice over Internet Protocol (VoIP), document sharing and manipulation, text chat). (p. 19)

The design of OFDR was guided by a desire to be user-centred (Tullis and Albert 2008), such that technology maximised functionality and usability, and did not detract from (but rather was conducive to) the mediation process. Additional objectives that guided the design process were ensuring the safety and security of all parties and their information.

The project management processes that monitored the system design were systematic and thorough, with planning for risk management procedures, weekly discussions, and a commitment to transparent and documented processes. The scope of the project plan was structured enough to provide measures for accountability while also enabling flexibility in responding to changes across time.

4.2.1 System Design and Features

There were five considerations identified as critical to the development of the OFDR capability:

- Client accessibility to the required technology
- Usability factors
- Reliability factors
- Evaluation of OFDR outcomes versus established methods of FDR (e.g. face to face, telephone)
- Potential leveraging of technology to extend and enhance current FDR processes

In ensuring that the technical specifications of the service suited the needs of RAQ staff and their clients, two communication technology integration companies were invited to formulate innovative concepts to meet the technical challenges of the OFDR project. As a result, a technological solution was ordered and delivered by January 2010, incorporating solutions of Web Conferencing, document sharing, flash-based video, text chat, secure access, audio conferencing, telephony, recording, and boardroom video.

As aforementioned, the flexibility built into the project management plan meant that lessons learned could be accommodated into the system with ease. For example, features of the technology that had not been previously accounted for were discovered and adapted into the system, such as the ability to email notes recorded online to the family dispute resolution practitioner (FDRP) at the conclusion of the session.

System Design Principles Smith and Martinez (2009) propose an analytic framework for dispute system design containing five elements that, when carefully considered during development and implementation, can enhance the quality and effectiveness of the system. These elements include articulating: the *goals* of the system, the *structure and processes* of the system, the *stakeholders* involved in and affected by the system, the financial and human *resources* available, and the evaluation plans in place to determine the *success* of the system. Amsler et al. (2020) later extend this framework by including a sixth element, *context and culture*, to acknowledge the way that the larger environment in which the system is embedded affects its uptake. A thorough consideration of the system design requires a clear statement of driving principles and thought processes behind development.

In the current project, the goal was to expand the OFDR market in Australia from TDRS to online-enhanced capabilities, including video-conferencing. The structure was aligned with the non-adversarial processes touted by mediation, with a specific focus on family-related disputes. A variety of stakeholders were targeted and engaged at different stages throughout the system design and implementation, as will be detailed later in this chapter. Project funding from the Attorney General's Office allowed for the stated objectives to be achieved, although constraints were noted in the project report, such as an inability to conduct randomized control trials. Regarding human resources, training programs for mediators and other OFDR affiliated administrative staff were developed and evaluated and pre-mediation sessions for clients were conceptualized. A methodical and systematic evaluation was conducted to assess the effectiveness of the pilot OFDR system, also to be described in more detail later in this chapter. Finally, the Australian context was considered ripe for OFDR following the success of its predecessor, the TDRS.

However, the development of the current OFDR project was underpinned by several other design principles:

- Granular Redundancy, which allows the continuity of service if any aspect of the technology is interrupted
- Common look and feel to ensure ease of accessibility and use
- Common Authentication Directory based on the Windows operating system
- Flexibility of System
- System Environment with RAQ which could fully incorporate the OFDR technology.

The system is able to be operated across most platforms (Windows, Mac, Linux, Solaria and others), and only requires an internet browser and connection, Adobe Flash Player, and a web camera. Testing with mobile devices has had some success, but further development and testing is required to ensure seamless use of OFDR technology on these platforms. As no special software is required to access online services except for an Internet browser, the costs associated with service use include only those required to access the internet and telephone, in addition to any service fees that may be charged by the TDRS. These costs are made transparent to clients through informed consent processes during service engagement.

Security Considerations Although the costs associated with system development could have been reduced further and the ease of usability could have increased by relying on existing online communication services (such as Skype), it was ultimately decided that the disadvantages outweighed the potential benefits. Specifically, products such as Skype are limited not only by their lack of flexibility in their interfaces but also in their weak security frameworks.

Extensive testing procedures were conducted prior to OFDR implementation to identify and address security concerns. One solution used to enhance the protection of user information involved the integration of a Secure Access Gateway (SAG) which provides secure and stream-lined access across all of the necessary systems. Clients are required to enter a secure username and password in order to gain access to the OFDR session, with their participation in the session then further verified by the FDRP. Passwords must also be changed upon first log-in. The first names of all participating parties are then made visible via an Attendee List on the meeting screen template, to demonstrate transparency.

Challenges encountered during the development of this secure online platform included the visibility of attendees' phone numbers and last names in the online meeting template, private conversations being enabled between clients, and the visibility of the FDRP's last name in RAQ-allocated email addresses. These challenges to safety have since been resolved, with surnames and phone numbers masked and the development of an OFDR administration account paired with a generic email address that is used by all online FDRPs to ensure professional anonymity. Steps were also taken to ensure that the practitioner has complete control over all system elements during the OFDR session. That is, the practitioner is able to customise the location, size, and presence of certain template features while also controlling interactions between attendees, including using online caucuses when appropriate.

4.3 OFDR Services and Processes

The resulting OFDR process adopted by RAQ involved a four-stage process: (1) Registration, (2) Intake, (3) Pre-OFDR Education, and (4) Online Family Dispute Resolution. This section will detail the procedures and technology-enabled tools available at each stage.

1. Registration Entry into the OFDR service is facilitated through registration with the TDRS. Prospective clients are assessed by a TDRS operator for suitability for mediation according to their presenting needs, with cases then either provided with alternative referral options or scheduled for an intake session at a later date. An additional entry point into the service is proposed through the TDRS website which would provide an alternative secure entry point for clients to access OFDR services, including pre-FDR education and other TDRS resources including Forms, Policies, and Information Sheets.

2. Intake At this stage, prospective clients are more thoroughly assessed by a FDRP for suitability to OFDR using a screening tool that was developed through the course of this project by the research team (to be described in greater detail later in this section). Intake can either be conducted over the phone or using web-based video-conferencing software but should remain consistent across all parties involved in the dispute. For the latter, an online 'lobby' template was developed in response to feedback from the staff evaluation that suggested that it would be preferable to not connect straight to live video with clients without first having the opportunity to talk individually with the client. The 'lobby' acts as a virtual waiting room and is accessed via a secure web-link and authentication procedure.

During intake, the FDRP discusses the FDR process in more detail and gathers information regarding the specific nature of the dispute in question. The 'Agreement to Participate in FDR' form is also introduced and explained to ensure that the client understands and is willing to comply with the rules of FDR. For video-conferencing intake meetings, the FDRP can also use this time to identify issues in the client's environment that may disrupt the OFDR session, such as the privacy and confidentiality of the space, the potential for background distractions to disrupt the session, and the quality of the lighting and room features for video clarity. These issues should be re-checked in the individual session before commencement of the joint OFDR meeting.

Screening Tool An automated client screening tool was developed to assist service staff to systematically select appropriate participants for the OFDR pilot project. Staff underwent training and testing practices to gain competence and confidence in using the tool prior to use with clients.

The survey assessed the clients' intention and ability to use OFDR as well as their suitability to use OFDR instead of remaining with a telephone-based service. The survey was developed in accordance with four key decision categories that were developed in collaboration between project teams:

- Motivation or desire to be involved in OFDR
- Technology access and capability
- Suitability of the client's home setup to ensure an OFDR-conducive environment
- Case requirements or conditions are such that OFDR is an appropriate option

A decision map was subsequently created to assist staff in making decisions on client suitability (see Fig. 4.1). Clients were not considered suitable to participate if they experienced too many technical difficulties, were not proficient in using the system, were not able to engage effectively with the interface and camera or had security/privacy concerns. In addition, as the current program was a pilot project, complex cases were not considered appropriate for inclusion in order to account for the initial strain on the mediator as they adjusted to the new technology which could potentially decrease the quality of service to the client. Complex cases included those that presented with domestic violence or high levels of conflict, clients who appeared agitated or upset, client requests for interpreters or other support persons, or multiple parties were involved.

The project team maintained a commitment to continuous improvement by collecting ongoing data regarding screening tool usability and the efficiency of

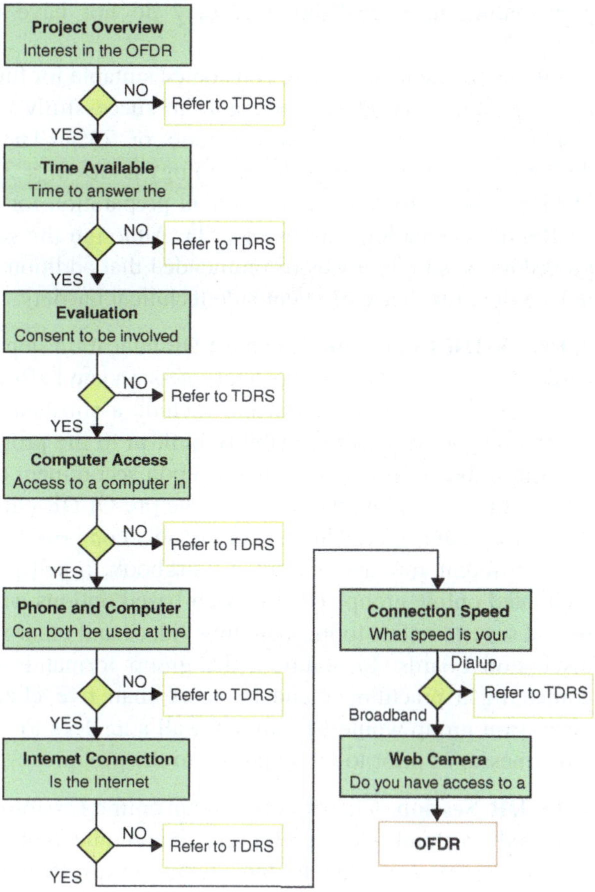

Fig. 4.1 Decision tree underlying the OFDR Client Screening Tool

related administration processes. An iterative design approach comprising both process, performance and subjective data (e.g., Kelkar et al. 2005) was adopted to ensure that revisions to the tool incorporated user feedback and recommendations.

An evaluation was conducted in September 2010 to determine effectiveness of the screening tool. A total of 54 qualitative comments were offered from clients who participated in the screening process but who were not deemed suitable for inclusion in the OFDR project. These data were analysed via categorisation into broader themes pertaining to the perceived barriers to participation. In order of prevalence, the responses provided by clients mentioned barriers to accessing technology (29.6%), accessing web-cams (25.9%), accessing reliable internet (14.8%), appointment scheduling conflicts (7.4%), perceived complexity of the process (5.5%), preference for non-visual communication (5.5%), problems concerning the other party (3.7%), and perceived level of personal effort required (1.95%). These results suggest that many clients engage in 'self-screening' and remove themselves from participating upon realising that they do not have the appropriate technology required.

Of the 30 clients who were considered suitable for further intake screening during this evaluation period, 22 were able to successfully complete the intake process, resulting in a screening success ratio of 73%. The remaining cases ($n = 8$) discontinued due to client-side technology issues ($n = 3$), non-arrival or cancellation of FDR process ($n = 2$), lack of client preparation for OFDR session ($n = 2$), and TDRS-side technology issues ($n = 1$). Although the success ratio of the screening procedure was high, it was recommended that additional screening be conducted to reduce the prevalence of client-side technical barriers.

3. Pre-OFDR Education The pre-FDR education step is to be completed after both parties have participated in the Intake session and before the FDR session. Although the original project scope did not include a substantial focus on developing and evaluating this stage, the flexibility built-in to the program design enabled for this element to become of larger interest upon securement of additional funding. At the time of the evaluation, the design of the pre-OFDR education program remained in the conceptual stages. The delivery of this component is proposed to be offered in three different formats: a printed workbook, a self-paced online resource, and a facilitated online group. The two web-based options would allow for the incorporation of several online tools, including videos and other visual materials, quizzes, and discussion boards. In addition, the group format is currently conceptualised as containing a practitioner and no more than five clients. The chat in the online discussion group would be public for all attendees to view, with the FDRP moderating messages prior to being posted to the group.

4. OFDR Session Clients access their online sessions through a unique web-link provided via email. These preliminary communications over email also provide links to a connection test whereby the clients can test their system settings against those required for the most efficient OFDR processes, in addition to a document containing frequently asked questions regarding navigation of the software.

The link provided directs the client to a virtual waiting room which is modelled on the same 'lobby' template described previously. The 'lobby' serves as an ideal starting point to an FDR session as it enables all participants to settle into the session in the least threatening or challenging experience. At the session time, the FDRP contacts the client via telephone and commences the session, moving them from the 'lobby' template and to the OFDR meeting template. The OFDR system provides flexibility to deliver online FDR sessions with or without videoconferencing and for sessions to be conducted jointly, by co-facilitation, shuttle, or with interpreters (including sign languages) and/or support people.

Features The features within the OFDR session template include:

- file-sharing and photo-sharing capabilities (particularly useful for uploading photos of children to reinforce shared goals and a child-focused process)
- desktop sharing

- shared viewing of RAQ and RA National documents via a resource database
- the ability to manage document printing
- confidential breakout rooms (for in-session caucuses and/or pre-session preparation)
- shared display of a dynamic agenda and agreement
- shared access to an electronic whiteboard
- the ability for the FDRP to e-mail themselves a copy of electronic notes made in the meeting room, including the agenda and agreement

The online template is comprised of a number of small windows or 'pods' containing each of these features. Three templates are available for the FDRP, each consisting of different features according to specific purposes:[1] a sharing template, discussion template, and collaboration template.

4.4 Testing and Training

Testing Heslop et al. (2001) use the term 'technology transfer' to refer to the process of moving technology from the development phase into organisational environments. Organisations utilise checklists in these scenarios to determine the viability and anticipated success of innovative new technologies. Consequently, the emphasis is on risk management and assessing the maturity of a particular innovation (i.e., readiness for implementation).

Readiness was assessed for both clients and staff and consisted of user (competence) and site (technical) readiness checklists. For staff, the user readiness checklist assessed user competency in delivering FDR services, knowledge of OFDR work-related procedures, confidence in using the OFDR system, and understanding of the new work processes involved in using OFDR. The site readiness checklist focused on the capability of site infrastructure to support the technology by addressing OFDR system readiness, work environment readiness, and support staff readiness.

A cyclical process of designing, testing, and revising was adopted as a form of risk management and the readiness-checking of the system to 'go live'. Pre-implementation testing identified a number of issues that required amendment prior to piloting of the OFDR system. Some of these issues were found to be under the control of the FDRP and related to adjustments to the user interface and physical environment to ensure optimal video feed quality.

Training It was acknowledged that the development of an OFDR system qualitatively changed practitioner and party engagement with the mediation process, as consistent with conceptualisation of ODR acting as a 'fourth party' to the mediation process (Katsh and Rifkin 2001). That is, OFDR capabilities are not isolated purely

---

[1]Refer to section 8.1 of report for more detail on the composition of these templates.

to the realm of the technical. Principles of human/computer interaction and consideration of changes to traditional FDR facilitation process within the online context require a systematic and integrated approach to the OFDR Pilot Project. As such, both FDRPs and front-line TDRS administration staff required specialised training to help manage the unique and added demands of using an OFDR service.

All TDRS administration staff completed training for orientation to the OFDR system and project, use of the registration tool and other administrative activities, and basic technical support to assist clients. The FDRP training was more exhaustive and covered use of the intake screening tool, use of the technology, FDR skills, and readiness and motivation to engage in the OFDR project. An evaluation of the training was conducted by the research team, with methodology and findings presented in Sect. 4.5.1.

4.5 Evaluation

To assess the effectiveness of the system against intended project objectives,[2] an extensive and methodologically rigorous research process was undertaken by the research team. Consistent with RAQ's commitment to evidence-based practice, the studies were designed to produce Category II- 2 evidence (that is, evidence from well-designed controlled trials without randomization; Harris et al. 2001).

The research team of two staff led a number of major initiatives and contributed to other activities involved in the design and implementation of the OFDR system, including: development of an intake screening tool, development and evaluating of staff training, work process mapping, acceptance testing, report writing, project management, and a participative action research project to engage with Aboriginal and Torres Strait Islander peoples. The main focus of the research team's involvement in the project, however, was on examining and documenting staff and client attitudes and responses to the OFDR system. This process consisted of data collection at seven different timepoints (refer to Fig. 4.2), the selection of which was informed by literature on dispute resolution program evaluation: Pre-Go Live Testing, Client Registration, Intake, Pre-OFDR information Session, OFDR Session, 3-Month Follow-Up, and 9-Month Follow-Up. The purpose of the 3- and 9-month follow-ups was to determine the impact of OFDR involvement on long-term outcomes. No information had been collected from the final two time-points[3] at the time of report submission. Therefore the remainder of this chapter will be dedicated to

---

[2]Refer to pp. 92–93 of report for questions used to guide the evaluation of the OFDR pilot project. Broadly, these questions targeted client experiences and expectations of the OFDR system, the effectiveness and efficiency of the OFDR system compared to other dispute resolution delivery modes, the usability of the system, the training needs of staff, the short and long-term impact of OFDR, and the effectiveness of pre-education OFDR.

[3]Refer to pp. 85–87 of report for methodology for these stages.

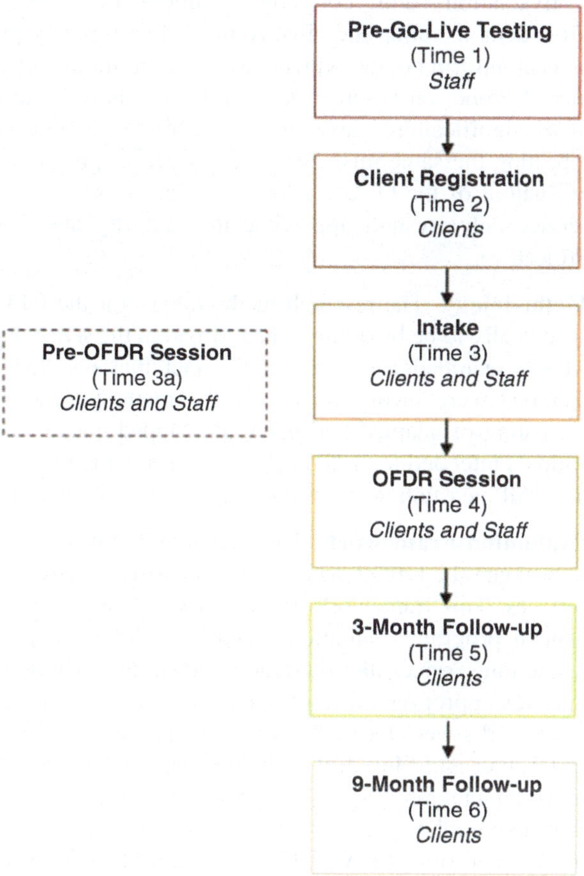

Fig. 4.2 Flowchart of OFDR pilot program evaluation process

detailing the processes and findings at each of the time points for which data are available.

Need for Evaluation Previous efforts at evaluating the efficacy and effectiveness of dispute resolution have suffered from a lack of thoroughness. For example, evaluations of dispute resolution have been criticised for adopting a narrow focus and utilisation of a limited range of measurement tools (Bailey and McCarty 2009; Hollett et al. 2002; Poitras and Le Tareau 2009). Determinants of mediation success are typically quantified by data such as service utilisation, frequency of resolution, and characteristics of the agreements reached during the session. In addition, a common mistake made by evaluators of mediation programs is the failure to consider both process and outcome; two distinct aspects that must be evaluated conjointly to provide an accurate picture of overall efficacy (Hollett et al. 2002; Kelly and Gigy 1988). Therefore, the evaluation of OFDR should address these shortcomings by adopting a thorough and systematic approach.

Evaluation—done correctly—is important on two broad levels (Small 1990). First, demonstrating the effectiveness of community programs increases awareness and can inform policy, which may result in funding opportunities for future endeavours. Second, an absence of rigorous evaluative data may force new programs to invest significant resources in "reinventing strategies that others found promising or repeating the same mistakes made by earlier programs" (Small 1990, p. 132). The evaluation of the OFDR pilot was vital in order to realise the potential of online service delivery and appreciate the integrity and rigour adopted by the OFDR Project.

Methodology The research methodology for the OFDR Evaluation was designed specifically to be broad and deep. Broad in the sense that a range of topics and times were researched and deep in the fact that detailed quantitative and qualitative methods were incorporated into the methodology. This mixed-methods design, consisting of adapted and newly developed questionnaires, interviews, and observations, intended to, and did, provide a rich picture of this human service intervention. All measures were psychometrically valid and empirically based.

Evaluation Framework The Research Team developed an integrated framework to evaluate the OFDR service in comparison to existing face-to-face and telephone services. This framework was informed by a review of the dispute resolution and general program evaluation literatures. Notwithstanding the longevity of dispute resolution services, the literature yielded minimal evidence of an evaluation model that was appropriate for both practice and research contexts. As such, two suitable frameworks were located from the literature (i.e., Jacobs' [1988] five-tiered model and Telfair and Mulvihill's [2000] Integrated Model of Community-Based Evaluation) and integrated[4] in order to inform the project management plan and identify key tasks to complete at each stage of the evaluation process. Moreover, OFDR-relevant process and outcome variables were identified from reviews of the dispute resolution, computer-mediated communication and information systems literatures, and discussions with internal subject matter experts. These outcome indicators were used to inform selection of evaluation tools and measures. The specific variables identified as relevant to the OFDR project are as follows:[5]

- Information quality and client preparedness for mediation
- Client beliefs regarding mediation effectiveness
- Trust in the organisation and OFDR technology
- Communication quality
- Quality of human-computer interaction (HCI) via the OFDR user interface
- Parental conflict and communication quality
- Interaction process
- Agreement quality

[4]Refer to Table 1 in report for the results of this integration.

[5]Refer to pp. 97–102 of report for summaries of each construct and its justification for inclusion into the current evaluation.

- Rapport
- Agreement compliance
- Client satisfaction

4.5.1 Time 1: Pre Go-Live Testing

The objective at this stage was to evaluate the use of the OFDR measures within a controlled environment. To this end, data were collected from staff to serve as baseline measures against which later data could be compared. Also conducted at this stage was staff pilot testing of all (i.e., both client and staff) evaluation measures that would be used in later stages of the implementation.

Due to the high failure rate of technology projects reported by the literature (Charette 2005; Emam and Koru 2008), it was considered essential that comprehensive pre-testing of the system components and the readiness and proficiency of staff who would ultimately have responsibility for using this system be conducted. Of the factors implicated in technology project failure, people- and process-related challenges are commonly cited (Kappleman et al. 2006). Specifically, senior management support, project management expertise, stakeholder consultation, clarity of project documentation, change control, and communications strategies are likely to influence the success of large-scale project implementations (Kappleman et al. 2006).

Individual factors may also impact on the implementation of new technologies. Scholars have warned against making the assumption that a high-level desire to change translates to readiness at the employee-level; "leaders tend to be particularly action oriented, and they react with impatience and frustration when their employees are not prepared to follow immediately" (Prochaska and Norcross 2001, p. 254).

Failure to match change implementation to employee readiness can be costly—potentially resulting in change failure and turnover (Prochaska and Norcross 2001). Moreover, individual characteristics such as openness (Judge et al. 1999; Vakola et al. 2004), organisational commitment (Judge et al. 1999; Vakola and Nikolaou 2005; Yousef 2000) and job satisfaction (Yousef 2000) create a particular context in which change occurs.

Informed by the literature, the research team adopted a planned approach to organisational change (Graetz et al. 2002; Waddell et al. 2007) which involved understanding:

- The organisational context for change
- Conducing a task/job analysis, and
- Individual-level consideration

To better understand the specific technical and hypothesised attitudinal requirements for successful participation in OFDR, the research team adapted a leading model of technology acceptance—the unified theory of acceptance and use of technology (UTAUT; Venkatesh et al. 2003). This extended model is comprised of eight constructs and intends to explore the relationships between OFDR-relevant attitudes and behavioural intention to adopt the system for both clients and staff:[6]

- Performance Expectancy
- Effort Expectancy
- Social Influence
- Facilitating Conditions
- Trust in Technology
- Trust in the TDRS
- Web Innovativeness
- Behavioural Intention

As overviewed in Chap. 3, the extended model of technology acceptance (with modifications) was validated within the staff population ($n = 127$; Casey and Wilson-Evered 2012). Staff attitudes toward technology such as perceived usefulness, ease of use, and the perceived influences of peers and management directly predicted behavioural intention to use OFDR. In addition, trust in both technology and the organisation, and web innovativeness, influenced behavioural intention indirectly via the mediating effects of core UTAUT constructs.

4.5.1.1 Organisational Context

Methodology Research suggests that staff attitudes (Mathieu et al. 1992; Noe and Schmitt 1986) and organisational context (Colquitt et al. 2000) can influence the effectiveness of technology acceptance. Therefore, an organisation-wide survey was designed and disseminated among staff to capture employee attitudes toward the implementation of OFDR technology. Interviews with FDRPs were also conducted to complement survey results.

Results Approximately 50% of the organisation responded to the survey ($n = 127$). Staff indicated a high level of job satisfaction and a commitment to change, however, aggregated attitudes toward the uptake of OFDR technology were less positive and more varied. An evaluation of the extended UTAUT model with a sample of staff also found that attitudinal factors accounted for 49.4% of the variance in OFDR adoption intentions.

Interviews with clinical practitioners ($n = 17$) revealed that just over a third held positive attitudes toward OFDR implementation. Concerns for the reliability and trust of the technology in addition to the need for adequate training were also common responses among interviewees, indicating a need to target these areas in particular to increase organisational support.

[6]Refer to p. 131 of report for explanation of each of these constructs.

4.5.1.2 Job Analysis

Methodology Job analysis (JA) is a widely employed (Morgeson and Campion 1997) method to define and/or clarify organisational positions. Typically, JA involves the collection of data on a particular job regarding the tasks and functions performed by incumbents, details of the organisation and working environment and responsibilities of the position (Arvey et al. 1977; Langeland et al. 1997; Maurer and Tarulli 1997). A job analysis methodology was employed in the OFDR evaluation to estimate anticipated changes to the existing FDRP role. These data then informed the training plan and implementation strategy. Seventeen interviews with FDRPs were conducted with corresponding data subject to thematic analysis.

Results Identified in the data was a need for training to incorporate the following components (listed in order of prevalence): technical training in the OFDR system, generic computer skills, FDR practice skills, organisational policies and procedures, and technical troubleshooting skills. Following the job analyses (and the development of OFDR technology), considerable effort was devoted to identifying the specific skills and tasks that are required to operate the system. This instrument was then used to inform the design of the training program.

4.5.1.3 Individual-Level Considerations

Training Plan Implementing new technologies can be difficult due to contextual and individual differences (Gattiker 1992). A user's prior experience, self-efficacy, technological familiarity, expectations (Compeau and Higgins 1995; Gravill and Compeau 2008), attitudes (Davis 1993; Taylor and Todd 1995), and even mood (Venkatesh and Speier 1999) may impact on implementation success. However, through careful training needs analysis, program design and change management, these challenges can be mitigated—producing greater technology uptake (Johnson and Marakas 2000). The data collected through staff interviews and the organisation-wide survey was integrated to perform a training needs analysis. Brief reviews of the adult education and technology training literatures further informed the training approach.

Supporting Evidence from the Literature As supported by the change management literature (Howell and Higgins 1990; Markham 1998), project 'champions' were selected to help rally support for projects and contribute to project success through their expertise and enthusiasm. Evidence on adult learning principles was also consulted to shape training program content, namely Knowles et al.' (2005) set of assumptions which have previously been found as useful when approaching the design and delivery of content in a range of organisational contexts (e.g., Birzer 2003; Milligan 1995). Finally, recommendations from the technology training literature were incorporated into the OFDR training plan,[7] which involved: using handouts, allocating time to practice skills, providing online self-paced modules, providing feedback to staff, and conducting role plays.

Training Needs Data collected from staff interviews and an organization-wide survey were integrated to help inform the design of these training program. Responses identified training needs in areas of: using video-conferencing software, interpreting non-verbal communication signals, software troubleshooting, and organisational processes and procedures in relation to OFDR services. Staff also indicated their preferred modes of OFDR training delivery, which involved experiential activities, ongoing mentoring and support, take-away resources and materials, structured sessions, and clear content.

Taken together, this evidence was used to develop a training program that consisted of a two-day class-based orientation training, followed by a series of smaller 'refresher' self-paced online modules. Day one focussed on the technical knowledge required to operate the OFDR system. Day two involved a series of role-plays and demonstrations that gave participants a realistic simulation of OFDR service delivery.

Evaluation Following each day of orientation training, participants were asked to complete an intra-training evaluation questionnaire which is a commonly used indicator of training effectiveness (Bassi et al. 1996). Results ($n = 6$) indicated that staff were satisfied with the training and gained increased confidence in OFDR technology use. Comparisons to pre-contemplation baseline survey data showed a general trend of increased technology acceptance post-training. Both qualitative comments and observational data (via the user readiness checklist) also supported survey data interpretations, showing that confidence appeared to increase across time and the experiential activities were found to be beneficial in learning.

Subsequent training sessions have used this training methodology and evaluation and continue to deliver positive results. This training method therefore appears to be an effective way to build capability among staff in using OFDR.

4.5.2 Time 2: Client Registration

Securing consumer perceptions of a new product or innovation can be useful to determine the likelihood of future uptake. Indeed, marketing scholars suggest that without market research, new products are more likely to fail (Crawford 1977). Moreover, some organisations mistakenly conduct consumer research after products have been developed—arguably, research should inform development (Brown and

[7]Refer to p. 159 of report for the application of technology training literature to the OFDR training program.

Eisenhardt 1995). Marketers of new products and services are encouraged to develop and conduct research at an early stage to ensure that differences between and within market segments informs product development (Goldenberg et al. 2001).

The prediction of information technology uptake has received significant attention from the research community. A key motivating factor behind this interest is the particularly high failure rate of IT implementations (Aiman-Smith and Green 2002; Kelly 2000; Lippert and Davis 2006; Markus 2004). Arguably, human factors have the potential to either 'make or break' IT projects (Lorenzi and Riley 2000). Market research can help to uncover factors that facilitate successful uptake and introduce new concepts to move individuals from 'pre-contemplation' toward change readiness (Prochaska and Norcross 2001).

Methodology Following registration for the TDRS service, clients were asked to participate in the pre-contemplation research survey. These baseline data were collected from clients to assist in longitudinal analyses of change once clients had engaged with the OFDR system. A rudimentary computer assisted telephone interviewing (CATI) system was developed to facilitate the collection of client data. Specifically, telephone information and referral officers verbally administered the OFDR pre-contemplation survey[8] and also obtained qualitative data through requests for general comments.

Results The final sample consisted of 621 usable responses, which represented a response rate of 13.17%. A substantial minority of these participants (14%) reported current or past instances of domestic violence with their partner. Regarding technology accessibility, participants identified access to web camera technology as more of a challenge than access to a personal computer or an internet connection, and 59% reported medium to fast internet connectivity speeds. Attitudes toward technology acceptance were largely favourable among respondents, with positive attitudes recorded toward system usefulness, system ease of use, trustworthiness of OFDR technology, and the influence of important others in encouraging technology uptake. However, of the 102 client comments analysed for affect, approximately half were neutral ($n = 27$, 26%) or negative ($n = 21$, 21%) reactions towards the system. The most prevalent themes among these comments[9] concerned communication quality ($n = 12$), time frames ($n = 10$), technological familiarity ($n = 8$), convenience ($n = 8$), and service quality ($n = 7$), indicating that these concerns are worthy of greater attention given the consensus among clients.

This analysis also revealed individual differences in preferences for method of service delivery although text-based chat was generally considered a poor method for communication. Several expectations were apparent for OFDR systems, namely personalisation of visual modalities, improved speed and efficiency in technology-enhanced services, and the accommodation of clients whose schedules

[8]Refer to pp. 76–78 of report for measures.

[9]Refer to p. 144 of report for a complete list of themes and examples.

require after-hours services. Perceived barriers to use identified by the clients included: gender, anticipated technical mastery required to use the OFDR system, regularity/comfort of Internet use, and complexity of the cases (particularly in relation to violence).

A number of suggestions regarding system development, implementation, and promotion were also raised by clients. Respondents typically suggested strategies to develop a 'user-friendly' system (i.e., adopting a simple user interface design) and to ensure that information is accessible (i.e., available to users and worded at a basic level of technical capability). Second, clients made suggestions regarding service promotion techniques—Centrelink was mentioned as a potential marketing venue by two respondents.

UTAUT Findings The extended UTAUT model was also validated with the client sample. A hierarchical regression analysis was conducted to determine the relative contributions of each predictor to the criterion measure—behavioural intention to use OFDR. The results of the statistical analysis indicated that clients' intentions to adopt OFDR may be influenced by attitudes toward the usefulness of OFDR, the perceived ease of use of the system, the influence of important others—and, to a lesser extent, access to sufficient knowledge and resources. Trust in OFDR technology and web innovativeness also emerged as significant predictors of Behavioural Intention. Surprisingly, trust in the TDRS was not a significant predictor of Behavioural Intention.

However, of those who reported the existence of domestic violence, preliminary data show that domestic violence may have a suppressing effect on clients' willingness to engage in OFDR. That is, follow-up correlation analyses showed that presence of domestic violence was negatively related to Behavioural Intention, Performance Expectancy, Effort Expectancy, and Facilitating Conditions.

4.5.3 Time 3: Intake

The purpose of the evaluation following intake was to collect data from staff and clients regarding their experiences of the session; specifically, the quality of human-computer interaction, client satisfaction, and the impact of technology on practice and process.

Methodology Clients completed a battery of measures[10] electronically at the conclusion of their intake session with an additional open-ended qualitative item for general comments. Staff also completed an electronic battery of measures and several qualitative items following their intake session.

[10]Refer to pp. 80–81 of report for client and staff measures.

Results During the period of evaluation, four FDRPs supplied evaluative data on 16 sessions and 19 clients supplied feedback data on their respective sessions. All of the 19 clients in the OFDR Post-Intake client survey group were from a non-Aboriginal and/or Torres Strait Islander background.

Staff Perceptions Staff indicated that the system was easy to use, of high aesthetic quality, and relevant for their practice. As compared with the TDRS, staff reported that the tools available (such as document sharing capabilities) increased the value of the service and visual cues enhanced rapport development. However, intakes were also considered to be more complex and time-consuming.

Additional challenges reported in using the OFDR system were experienced during a significant minority of the sessions, including technical difficulties (e.g., lagging videos, web-cam functioning), FDR practice (e.g., maintaining direct eye contact, forgetting to use available tools, needing to pay attention to personal non-verbal behaviours, low initial confidence), and administrative activities (e.g., an excess of emails sent to clients, having to complete administrative activities in-session, reiterating appropriate client behaviours pre-session). Staff recommended that assistance from IT support be available during the sessions to resolve technical difficulties as they occur.

Client Perceptions Overall, clients reported favourable impressions of using the technology and interacting with the systems. Though satisfaction was just over moderate, all other scales suggested that users were well prepared, they trusted the technology, and they found the experience to be highly positive. The visual quality of the OFDR system was rated favourably by clients with reports that the interface was easy to navigate. Despite concerns that the OFDR system would interfere with the development of rapport, clients reported that professional relationships were well established. Clients also reported a willingness to use the OFDR system again.

Responses to open-ended comments revealed that clients found the process trustworthy due to the inclusion of visual elements, which they also found increased perceptions of confidentiality. There were also some technical challenges reported, including poor video feed quality, lost video connection, and discomfort due to holding the telephone handset for an hour.

4.5.4 Time 4: Pre-FDR Education Session

It is a requirement of the FDR process in Australia that disputing parties complete an informational preparatory session prior to the commencement of mediation. Parents have reported in past research studies that FDR information sessions are very helpful in preparing them for the mediation process (Blaisure and Geasler 1996; Brandon 2006; Mathis et al. 1999). In addition, mediators have also reported, in an American nationwide survey, that pre-mediation education sessions make parents more child-focused in mediation compared to parents who had not gone through the same education process (Arbuthnot and Kramer 1998).

Kitzmann et al. (2012)[11] have claimed that several interrelated factors have spurred an increase in the development of specialized programs which prepare parents to engage in the mediation process:

- Mediation preparation programs may increase the likelihood that parents will go on to reach an agreement in mediation.
- These programs can provide the foundation for parents to establish and maintain a successful co-parenting relationship, one which can shelter the child from conflict during and after the mediation process.

In their subsequent review of mediation preparation programs, Kitzmann and colleagues found that very few programs have been evaluated, meaning that little is known about these programs' effectiveness. Whilst there is much research on methods for the FDR process, there is little research on whether the parties are actually ready to enter the process.

Although the development of pre-OFDR education sessions remained in the conceptualisation stage at the time of the RAQ OFDR pilot program, it was considered important to evaluate current modes of pre-FDR education delivery to help inform the design of the new format while also contributing to the knowledge base on pre-FDR program effectiveness. As such, the research team conducted evaluations of FDR Group Information Sessions at three Queensland Family Relationship Centres (FRC) in February 2011. Data were collected pertaining to the content and process of the sessions as well as general client feedback and satisfaction levels.

Methodology A mixed-methods design was adopted by gathering quantitative data through client evaluation surveys[12] and qualitative data through three different methods: (1) interviews with the Senior FDR Clinical Leader, (2) thematic analysis of the handouts provided to clients during the sessions, and (3) observations of 20 FDR information sessions across three locations (Upper Mount Gravatt, Strathpine, and Cairns). The duration of each session was approximately one and a half hours and the average class size was five participants. The data from these locations were then compared against each other to identify similarities and differences that occurred across programs.

The data collection procedure for the quantitative evidence followed a pre-post design whereby participants completed pre-measures at the beginning of the FDR Information Session and the post-measures at the conclusion of the session. This design allowed for the assessment of changes across time in knowledge, attitudes, and behavioural intentions as a function of session participation.

---

[11] Ainsworth et al. (2017).

[12] Refer to pp. 212–215 of report for measures.

Results Five core content themes were observed to be common across all 20 sessions:

- Adults and Separation—the grief process
- Children and Separation—effects of conflict and separation on children
- Models of Co-parenting—Conflict, Parallel, Co-operative
- FDR Process and Steps—preparation for mediation
- Referrals to other contacts and services in the back on the workbook

The workbook and session content were found to be similar across all programs, with an emphasis on child-focused processes. Session content differed minimally as a function of the facilitator's professional background, although a common observation was that facilitators who used micro-counselling skills appeared to involve clients more in discussion and make clients feel more at ease. Some venues varied in their use of media and methods of communicating information, however, there was a notable absence of skill-building activities.

Sixty-seven participants completed the surveys. At pre-test, the majority (58.7%) of participants indicated that they preferred the facilitated group session format as compared to alternative delivery methods. Reasons provided for this preference included: the ability to ask questions, the intimacy of face-to-face delivery, and the ability to engage in discussion with others who have shared experiences. Participants also rated their self-care and general well-being fairly high.

Comparisons across time found that participants reported mixed and subtle changes in terms of preparedness while confidence regarding mediation remained fairly stable despite the intervention. Notably, participants reported increases across all areas of learning and many areas of prosocial co-parenting skills, thereby demonstrating the effectiveness of a brief intervention. Participants also showed high levels of agreement that both the facilitator's approach to managing the session and its goals and objectives were met.

Participants reported enjoying the following elements of the sessions: the videos selected; the focus on the child; the support of the group; that the content was easy to understand; having the ability to ask questions; and obtaining information about the FDR process. There were mixed responses regarding the length of the sessions and the relevance of the content to individual situations. Problems identified with the program and subsequent recommendations for improvements included: more time for discussion; remove survey from in-session completion; using more practical examples and tools; consideration of group composition; and acknowledgement and management of emotions.

4.5.5 Time 5: OFDR Session

Post-OFDR session data were collected from both clients and staff to understand the quality of human-computer interaction, client satisfaction and the impact of technology on practice and process.

Methodology At the conclusion of the OFDR sessions, both clients and FDRPs completed a battery of measures[13] with several qualitative questions included. At the time of report submission, only four OFDR sessions had been completed with client data forthcoming, although preliminary qualitative feedback was obtained with two clients via telephone interviews. Two FDRPs provided data on two of these sessions, with a further two sessions being observed by the research team.

Results The FDRPs reported no practitioner-side technical difficulties with the OFDR system and no difficulties engaging in FDR practice during the session. They also reported that the OFDR administration process was efficient and easy to use, however the involvement of a co-facilitator may be beneficial when learning the system (one to focus on technology and one to focus on mediation practice). Additional recommendations from the FDRPs include to pre-empt and plan strategies to manage technical issues prior to the mediation session.

Regarding client feedback, the response was largely positive even though neither case reached an agreement by the end of the session. Both clients reported good rapport with their respective FDRPs. One client experienced no technical difficulties while another experienced minor connectivity issues. Overall, both clients and staff reported high levels of satisfaction with the OFDR system.

4.6 Recommendations

Following from the learnings over the course of the development and evaluation of an OFDR system, a number of recommendations can be proposed to guide future research and practice, as summarised below:

- Development of an OFDR technical solution that ensures a secure, safe and controlled online space requires consideration of specific System Design Principles (as noted in Sect. 4.2.1).
- Installation and customization of the technology must prioritise security of information shared in the online environment to ensure privacy of client data and the ability to withhold confidential information.
- Resources need to be allocated to enable the ongoing investigation and review of current and emerging technologies to remain current and relevant for the intended client group.

[13]Refer to p. 83 of report for measures.

- System design should continuously consider the cost to the end user.
- Development and promotion of the technology needs to support ease and confidence of client engagement as well as etiquette and ground rules for the online environment.
- Consideration must be given to the complexity of the online environment and detailed guidelines should be developed to include all aspects of the online service for clients. These should include for example a consideration of transparency, the sharing of documents, email protocol, photo sharing and confidentiality.
- The consideration of both practice and technical issues is required in considering layout and design for the online sessions.
- Screening processes for clients involved in an online service need to include client readiness and appropriateness.
- Staff training and readiness for online services is essential for the successful roll-out of online service delivery.
- The design of an OFDR system should aim to promote a sense of trust in technology, in particular a high rate of reliability and promoting privacy and confidentiality provisions.
- Staff training could be supplemented with mentors or coaches to assist in skill maintenance for all staff, and the development of super users to play the role of help desk, troubleshooting roles.
- Pre-FDR Education should be part of the OFDR model.

4.7 Conclusion

Overall, the results are promising; in general, both staff and clients are motivated and able to use on line technologies for service delivery. Technology-enabled services can reach further, have a wider range of resources and be accessed by more people through systems such as OFDR. The evidence presented in this evaluation supports arguments that the technology has benefits in terms of ease of access, ease of use, being trustworthy and readily available in the hands of skilled and experienced practitioners. Dissemination of resources, information, and programs using online platforms appears to be an advantageous avenue to service access as it meets a need in the Australian community as indicated by the willingness for continued use.

The highly thorough and systematic approach to development and evaluation that was employed in the current pilot project increase confidence in claims that these provide beneficial outcomes for users. Further, extensive testing and trialling of the technology prior to implementation resulted in minimal technical difficulties being experienced from both staff and clients. As such, the brief training (for staff) and education (for clients) sessions appeared adequate to prepare users for engaging with the system. Of particular importance is the opportunity to allow prospective users to engage with the system prior to formal use through a hands-on practical demonstration.

As such, not only has this evaluation provided evidence of the utility of online adaptations for family dispute resolutions, but it has also contributed to the knowledge base by detailing best-practice for the development of OFDR systems. The lessons learned from this extensive process can thereby be used to guide future OFDR development:

- Provide additional training to staff using video feedback on non-verbal and verbal behaviours.
- Precontemplation research is useful in helping to develop targeted communications.
- Developing new work methods, communication systems, and processes could encourage client up-take.
- As clients are highly experienced in using online systems, staff should be equally experienced.
- Host organisations need to have adequate levels of sophistication in their ICT systems and infrastructures, users, interface development, speed, and back up processes.
- Specifications grounded in service delivery requirements need to be articulated from all perspectives at the outset of the contract.
- The interface design should be guided by a variety of perspectives reflecting different needs, including end users from practice, training, client services, quality, risk management and security, user interface specialists, and be grounded in functional requirements.
- Using project management methodologies is essential.
- Technology testing with the vendor is critical for success.
- Evaluation must be factored into the project concept development and design and endorsed by senior management in project plans.
- Develop and test effective communications with clients to ensure readiness for engagement.

References

Aiman-Smith L, Green SG (2002) Implementing new manufacturing technology: the related effects of technology characteristics and user learning activities. Acad Manag J 45:421–430

Ainsworth N, Zeleznikow L, Zeleznikow J (2017) Readiness for family dispute resolution – an examination of how education helps prepare disputing parents to negotiate their conflicts. Paper presented at the International Association for Conflict Management, Berlin, Germany

Amsler LB, Martinez JK, Smith SE (2020) Dispute system design. Stanford University Press, Menlo Park

Arbuthnot J, Kramer K (1998) Effects of divorce education on mediation process and outcome. Mediat Q 15:199–213

Arvey RD, Passino EM, Lounsbury JW (1977) Job analysis results as influenced by sex of incumbent and sex of analyst. J Appl Psychol 62:411–416

Bailey J, McCarty D (2009) Assessing empowerment in divorce mediation. Negot J 25:327–336

Bassi LJ, Benson G, Cheney S (1996) The top ten trends. Train Dev 50. https://www.questia.com/magazine/1G1-18957341/the-top-ten-trends

Birzer ML (2003) The theory of andragogy applied to police training. Policing: An Int 26:29–42

Blaisure KR, Geasler MJ (1996) Results of a survey of court-connected parent education programs in U.S. counties. Fam Court Rev 34:23–40
Brandon D (2006) Can four hours make a difference? Evaluation of a parent education program for divorcing parents. J Divorce Remarriage 45:171–185
Brown S, Eisenhardt K (1995) Product development: past research, present findings and future directions. Acad Manag Rev 20:343–378
Casey T, Wilson-Evered E (2012) Predicting uptake of technology innovations in online family dispute resolution services: an application and extension of the UTAUT. Comp Hum Behav 28:2034–2045
Charette RN (2005) Why software fails. IEEE Spectrum, 2 September. https://spectrum.ieee.org/computing/software/why-software-fails
Colquitt JA, LePine JA, Noe RA (2000) Toward an integrative theory of training motivation: a meta-analytic path analysis of 20 years of research. J Appl Psychol 85:687–707
Compeau D, Higgins C (1995) Computer self-efficacy: development of a measure and initial test. MIS Q 19:189–211
Crawford C (1977) Marketing research and the new product failure rate. J Market 41:51–61
Davis F (1993) User acceptance of information technology: system characteristics, user perceptions and behavioural impacts. Int J Man-Mach Stud 38:475–487
Emam K, Koru A (2008) A replicated survey of IT software project failures. IEEE Softw 25:84–90
Gattiker UE (1992) Computer skills acquisition: a review and future directions for research. J Manag 18:547–574
Goldenberg J, Libai B, Muller E (2001) Talk of the network: a complex systems look at the underlying process of word-of-mouth. Market Lett 12:211–233
Graetz F, Rimmer M, Lawrence A, Smith A (2002) Managing organisational change. Wiley, Milton
Gravill J, Compeau D (2008) Self-regulated learning strategies and software training. Inf Manag 45:288–296
Harris RP, Helfand M, Woolf SH, Lohr KN, Mulrow CD, Teutsch SM, Atkins D (2001) Current methods of the U.S. Preventive Services Task Force: a review of the process. Am J Prev Med 20 (3 Suppl):21–35
Heslop LA, McGregor E, Griffith M (2001) Development of a technology readiness assessment measure: the cloverleaf model of technology transfer. J Technol Transf 26(4):369–384
Hollett N, Herrman M, Eaker D, Gale J (2002) The assessment of mediation outcome: the development and validation of an evaluative technique. Just Syst J 23:345–365
Howell JM, Higgins CA (1990) Champions of technological innovation. Admin Sci Q 35:317–341
Jacobs F (1988) The five-tiered approach to evaluation: context and implementation. In: Weiss H, Jacobs F (eds) Evaluating family programs. Aldine deGruyter, Hawthorne, pp 37–68
Johnson RD, Marakas GM (2000) The role of behavioral modeling in computer skills acquisition: toward refinement of the model. Inf Syst Res 11:402–417
Judge TA, Thoresen CJ, Pucik V, Welbourne TM (1999) Managerial coping with organizational change: a dispositional perspective. J Appl Psychol 84:107–122
Kappleman LA, McKeeman R, Zhang L (2006) Early warning signs of it project failure: the dominant dozen. Inf Syst Manag 23:31–36
Katsh E, Rifkin J (2001) Introducing the fourth party: the critical role of technology. In: Online dispute resolution: resolving conflicts in cyberspace. Jossey-Bass, San Francisco, pp 93–116
Kelkar K, Khasawneh MT, Bowling SR, Gramopadhye AK, Melloy BJ, Grimes L (2005) The added usefulness of process measures over performance measures in Interface design. Int J Hum-Comput Interact 18:1–18
Kelly J (2000) Children's adjustment in conflicted marriage and divorce: a decade review of research. J Am Acad Child Adolesc Psychiatry 39:963–973
Kelly J, Gigy L (1988) Measuring clients' perceptions and satisfaction. Confl Resolut Q 19:43–52
Kitzmann KM, Parra GR, Jobe-Shields L (2012) A review of programs designed to prepare parents for custody and visitation mediation. Fam Court Rev 50:128–136

Knowles MS, Holton EF, Swanson RA (2005) The adult learner: the definitive classic in adult education and human resource development. Taylor & Francis Ltd, Boston
Langeland KL, Johnson CM, Mawhinney TC (1997) Improving staff performance in a community mental health setting. J Organ Behav Manag 18:21–43
Lippert S, Davis M (2006) A conceptual model integrating trust into planned change activities to enhance technology adoption behavior. J Inf Sci 32:434–448
Lorenzi NM, Riley RT (2000) Managing change: an overview. J Am Med Inform Assoc 7:116–124
Markham SK (1998) A longitudinal examination of how champions influence others to support their projects. J Prod Innov Manag 15:490–504
Markus M (2004) Technochange management: using IT to drive organizational change. J Inf Technol 19:4–20
Mathieu JE, Tannenbaum SI, Salas E (1992) Influences of individual and situational characteristics on measures of training effectiveness. Acad Manag J 35:828–847
Mathis RD, Tanner Z, Whinery F (1999) Evaluation of participant reactions to premediation group orientation. Mediat Q 17:153–159
Maurer TJ, Tarulli BA (1997) Managerial work, job analysis, and Holland's RIASEC vocational environment dimensions. J Vocat Behav 50:365–381
Milligan F (1995) In defence of andragogy. Nurse Educ Today 15:22–27
Morgeson FP, Campion MA (1997) Social and cognitive sources of potential inaccuracy in job analysis. J Appl Psychol 82:627–655
Noe RA, Schmitt N (1986) The influence of trainee attitudes on training effectiveness: test of a model. Personnel Psychol 39:497–523
Poitras J, Le Tareau A (2009) Quantifying the quality of mediation agreements. Negot Confl Manag Res 2:363–380
Prochaska JO, Norcross JC (2001) Stages of change. Psychother Theory Res Pract Train 38:443–448
Relationships Australia (2011) Development and evaluation of online family dispute resolution capabilities. https://www.ag.gov.au/Publications/Pages/OnlineFamilyDisputeResolutionEvaluation.aspx
Small S (1990) Some issues regarding the evaluation of family life education programs. Fam Rel 39:132–135
Smith S, Martinez J (2009) An analytic framework for dispute systems design. Harv Negot Law Rev 14:123–169
Taylor S, Todd P (1995) Understanding information technology usage: a test of competing models. Inf Syst Res 6:144–176
Telfair J, Mulvihill BA (2000) Bridging science and practice: the integrated model of community-based evaluation. J Community Pract 7:37–65
Thomson M (2011) Alternative modes of delivery for family dispute resolution: the Telephone Dispute Resolution Service and the online FDR project. J Fam Stud 17:253–257
Tullis T, Albert B (2008) Measuring the user experience. Elsevier, Burlington
Vakola M, Nikolaou I (2005) Attitudes towards organizational change: what is the role of employees' stress and commitment? Empl Relat 27:160–174
Vakola M, Tsaousis I, Nikolaou I (2004) The role of emotional intelligence and personality variables on attitudes toward organisational change. J Manag Psychol 19:88–110
Venkatesh V, Speier C (1999) Computer technology training in the workplace: a longitudinal investigation of the effect of mood. Org Behav Hum Decis Process 79:1–28
Venkatesh V, Morris M, Davis G, Davis F (2003) User acceptance of information technology: towards a unified view. MIS Q 27:425–478
Waddell D, Creed A, Cummings TG, Worley C (2007) Contemporary management. McGraw-Hill, North Ryde
Yousef DA (2000) Organizational commitment: a mediator of the relationships of leadership behavior with job satisfaction and performance in a non-western country. J Manag Psychol 15:6–24

Chapter 5
Engaging Indigenous Peoples in Technology Supported Human Service Offerings

Abstract Loss of historical artefacts arising from colonisation and past social policy continue to cause disadvantage and distress for indigenous peoples all over the world and particularly so in Australia. Social efforts to improve community and family outcomes show little progress despite investment. The provision of culturally appropriate, high quality services could be enhanced through the use of technology, particularly in remote areas. One such application is the development of online options for family dispute resolution services. This study forms part of one example of community collaboration to ensure high quality, culturally appropriate services are available to some of the most disadvantaged groups in Australia. Using an organisational development approach via participatory action research, this chapter details an exercise in community engagement in planning for roll out of services. Data included both focus groups and researcher reflections which were pooled and analysed leading to the development of key themes. Participating communities appear ready and enthused by the concept of online service delivery; however, were wary of service provision that was not tailored to their needs or culturally insensitive. With ongoing modification and consultation with community reference groups, the service could be contextualised and adapted to better suit local needs.

5.1 Introduction

Historical artefacts arising from colonisation and past social policy continue to cause disadvantage and distress for Aboriginal and Torres Strait Islander people (Eades 2000; Faulkner 2015; Hunter 2003). There is potential for further erosion of the continent's first nations and their cultures through exposure to Western society (Varan 1998) impacting the cultural, social, mental and physical wellbeing of Aboriginal and Torres Strait Islander people, families and communities (Commonwealth of Australia 2017). Given the remote locations of many Aboriginal and Torres Strait Islander communities, high quality family and social services are often unavailable. This chapter documents a process of seeking consumer engagement in the early stages of service design that is culturally and contextually

E. Wilson-Evered, J. Zeleznikow, *Online Family Dispute Resolution*, Law, Governance and Technology Series 45,
https://doi.org/10.1007/978-3-030-64645-5_5

appropriate for a sensitive yet essential area, family dispute resolution (FDR). Specifically, the creation of an online family dispute resolution (OFDR) system for Aboriginal and Torres Strait Islander people in three different communities in Queensland, Australia.

In tailoring services specifically for Indigenous people of Queensland, we first recognised that in many aspects, the intended consumer base differed from non-Indigenous Australians in ways that need to be considered. To illustrate, the most recent Census data available (ABS 2012) indicates that in 2011 56% of Aboriginal and Torres Strait Islander peoples reported a combined household income of between $200 and $799 with only 13% reporting a single income over $1000 per week. The same report indicated that 6% of Aboriginal and Torres Strait Islander people lived in multiple family households (and was increasing slightly). Of the single family households, 29% were one parent families with dependent children (one or more). Finally, the report showed an increasing trend for access to the internet with 63% of households reporting an internet connection, up from 40% in 2006, although still below the reported rate for non-Indigenous households (84%). As such Aboriginal and Torres Strait Islander people are more likely than other Australians to have a lower income, live in a multiple family household or single parent household and are still less likely to have internet connection. Each of these aspects will have implications for use of FDR services and therefore should be considered in developing an OFDR product.

Services available to disadvantaged groups are often situated in the main capital cities or larger regional hubs which are inaccessible to many Aboriginal and Torres Strait Islander peoples. When services are provided they may not address the range of problems, needs and concerns of Aboriginal and Torres Strait Islander consumers. Consumers may access up to 20 services which rarely take a holistic view of the consumer and their family, an approach considered vital for Aboriginal and Torres Strait Islander peoples (Reeve and Bradford 2014). Online services have been shown to offer opportunities to extend the reach and range of services provided to Aboriginal and Torres Strait Islander communities in urban, regional and remote Australia (Radoll 2014; Thomson 2011). Despite considerable research interest in cross-cultural technology design, scant work is available that elucidates principles relevant to Aboriginal and Torres Strait Islander people—particularly in the area of virtual community services. Therefore, our research represents a unique and valuable opportunity to contribute to this body of knowledge while also addressing local community needs and promoting empowerment through a participatory action research (PAR) methodology. In this paper, we explore the intersections between culture and technology, and report on our tentative first steps in engaging with communities to design services to meet cultural and contextual needs.

Historically the impact of culture has not been central in the development of new technologies—implying the characteristics of user interaction are consistent across cultural groups, while more contemporary understanding reveals the importance of culture in these interactions (Frandsen-Thorlacius et al. 2009; Khaddam and Vanderdonckt 2014; Markus and Kitayama 1991; Noiwan and Norcio 2006). There is now a push for technologies that can adapt to users with different culturally influenced preferences (Khaddam and Vanderdonckt 2014; Reinecke and Bernstein 2013). Consequently, considering the culture of the intended user in the design, evaluation and marketing of technological innovations is vital (Jagne and Smith-Atakan 2006; Rainey 2012; Rao 2004; Reinecke and Bernstein 2013).

Within Australia, technological diffusion across cultural groups faces many challenges. In particular, Aboriginal and Torres Strait Islander communities experience significant disadvantage in comparison to the general population across a number of social determinants; for example, health, education, exposure to violence and access to technological infrastructure (ABS 2002, 2012). While the biannual *Closing the Gap* report has sought to address some of these inequalities since 2008, the most recent publication (2017) indicates most targets are not on track to be achieved by the envisaged time. Giving Aboriginal and Torres Strait Islander people more input into how best to address these inequalities may provide better outcomes (Turner 2017). In addition to the social and health differences, Australia's *digital divide* creates marked geographic, social, psychological and socio-economic barriers to the uptake of technology among regional and remote Aboriginal and Torres Strait Islander communities (Cullen 2001; Daly 2006). National strategies to improve access (Conroy 2010), have had some success, evidenced by a reported increase in Aboriginal and Torres Strait Islander people living in a household with internet connection between 2006 and 2011 (ABS 2012). Despite the increase this is still below the level of non-Indigenous residents. Technology acceptance is contingent on access to resources and the successful resolution of barriers stemming from the human computer interface, including culturally influenced preferences (Dyson 2002, 2003; Khaddam and Vanderdonckt 2014; Reinecke and Bernstein 2013).

This chapter describes one part of an ongoing program of research that aims to inform the co-design, implementation, promotion and practice model for an innovative online mediation, education and counselling service under development by a major not-for-profit family relationship service provider. First, the context of the project is described, including the research objectives that guided the development of our approach. Second, we describe the general PAR process and give a brief outline of the historical context of research involving Aboriginal and Torres Strait Islander communities. A description of the specific methodology adopted for this research follows. Finally, the results and implications of the research are discussed.

5.2 Project Context

In mid-2009, the Federal Attorney-General's Department commissioned the not-for-profit organisation Relationships Australia Queensland (RAQ) to conduct a pilot implementation study of OFDR. The project involves the design, implementation and evaluation of an OFDR system using a combination of staff and client samples. FDR was originally developed in New Zealand in response to criticisms that the existent child protection model did not adequately consider Maori culture and communities (Petrie and Kruger 2014). Briefly, FDR involves the mediation of parenting disputes by a neutral third party. Agreements between parents are negotiated with reference to the best interests of the children. Amendments to the Family Law Act in 2006 have sought to promote FDR as a viable alternative to the traditional adversarial approach characterised by litigation. FDR and OFDR have demonstrated good outcomes and have attracted national and international interest (Petrie and Kruger 2014; Thomson 2011). FDR has already shown to be beneficial for Aboriginal and Torres Strait Islander peoples in Australia's Northern Territory (Petrie and Kruger 2014). An OFDR system to provide relevant, high quality services to those outside major cities where mediation professionals primarily reside is the next important step.

Toward the end of 2009, our research team commenced a sub-project titled: "Cultural Considerations in Online Family Dispute Resolution." The purpose of this project was to develop an understanding of Aboriginal and Torres Strait Islander cultures and areas of current social, physical, mental and technological disadvantages. We hoped to utilise what we learned as we worked with local potential consumers in developing the OFDR. The project was borne out of the premise that technology is an artefact of the culture in which it is produced (Demeester 1999). Essentially, this position argues that characteristics of technology—such as iconography (Olson and Olson 2003), media (Dyson 2002), language (Parmaxi and Zaphiris 2016; Tractinsky 2000) and methods of interaction are influenced by culture (Khaddam and Vanderdonckt 2014; Onibere et al. 2001; Rainey 2012; Rao 2004). These characteristics may therefore lead to usability shortcomings or lack of adoption if they have not been tailored to suit the context and preferences of its users. In relation to the OFDR project, this realisation prompted our group to explore the relationships between technology design, promotion and implementation, and the subsequent likelihood of system uptake among Aboriginal and Torres Strait Islander communities. We sought to develop an appreciation of the versatility offered by OFDR to address local community needs.

In stage one of this project, we sourced extant knowledge among Aboriginal and other leaders, academic literature, white papers and reports from Government and State organisations who have taken this journey before us. Following a brief review of the technology acceptance, human-computer interaction and general Aboriginal and Torres Strait Islander literatures, we produced a comprehensive report and presented the findings to the organisation. During the discussions that followed, a number of action steps were proposed. The organisation supported further research to increase the cultural appropriateness of future online services. Several research objectives were proposed:

1. Develop further practical understanding of culturally-appropriate models of family mediation
2. Identify a collaborative research methodology that could be adopted in future projects involving Aboriginal and Torres Strait Islander communities
3. Establish networks and relationships with Aboriginal and Torres Strait Islander communities

4. Inform the development of a culturally-appropriate OFDR system that promotes effective human-computer interaction and user experiences.

The second phase of the project began the process of consultation and collaboration with a range of Aboriginal and Torres Strait Islander communities. The research team partnered with the Director of Aboriginal and Torres Strait Islander Programs to assist with the conceptualisation and preliminary planning and implementation of this process and the Director of Virtual Services to engage in the PAR process. Local internal stakeholders, primarily Aboriginal and Torres Strait Islander staff and key Zone Directors were also engaged to assist with the identification of relevant participants and community representatives.

The team elected to include three research sites to cover urban (Ipswich/Eight Mile Plains), regional (Townsville) and remote (Thursday Island) locations and communities. These locations represented a variety of cultural groups and provided a range of levels of social and economic disadvantage and social needs. Participants included both local Aboriginal (Ipswich, Eight Mile Plains, Townsville) and Torres Strait Islander (Eight Mile Plains, Townsville, Thursday Island) who shared perspectives and offered advice throughout the consultative process.

5.3 The Historical Context of Research Involving Indigenous Peoples

Historically, research involving Aboriginal and Torres Strait Islander peoples tended to adopt a top-down or directive approach, which created tension between researchers and communities (Branas and Gooda 2006; Henry et al. 2004). These effects are still being felt today; research can convey negative, paternalistic and colonisation connotations given the exploitative histories experienced by Aboriginal and Torres Strait Islander communities (Commonwealth of Australia 2017; Faulkner 2015; Humphrey 2001; Miller et al. 2015). However, past conflict over research processes and outputs has positively influenced the evolution of research practices (Henry et al. 2004), leading to the rising popularity of Participatory Action Research (PAR) as an appropriate methodology for engaging in research with Aboriginal and/or Torres Strait Islander communities (Davies 2007; Miller et al. 2015; Rigney 2006).

Although PAR is based on principles of collaboration, consultation, mutual ownership and empowerment of local people, the perception of traditional research by Indigenous communities can form an obstacle to initial entry and engagement. Specifically, First Nations' people may interpret research, based on negative prior experiences, as "something done to them for the benefit of outsiders, and from which they themselves receive no gain" (Dickson and Green 2001, p. 472). A common characteristic of PAR implementation is to spend time initially developing a relationship with the local people (Dickson and Green 2001; Miller et al. 2015), with the intention of building equal ownership and investment in the project over the long-term (Humphrey 2001). Therefore, a PAR methodology lends itself well to the culturally-appropriate conduct of research with Aboriginal and Torres Strait Islander people (Miller et al. 2015).

Recently, PAR has been adopted by researchers involved in cross-cultural work as a method of producing knowledge and action while retaining empirical rigour (e.g., Fine 2014; McIntyre 2003; Miller et al. 2015; Tsey et al. 2007). Without a genuine commitment to the values espoused by PAR, research involving diverse populations is less likely to succeed (Tsey et al. 2007). We drew on this body of work to inform the development of our culturally-appropriate methodology and engagement strategy, which focussed on close collaboration and establishment of ongoing research partnerships with local communities (Matthews and Burton 2013; Miller et al. 2015; Tsey et al. 2007).

5.4 Ethical Considerations

Cross-cultural researchers are bound by principles and guidelines of ethical conduct. As participatory research frameworks are implemented with increasing regularity, scholars involved with Aboriginal and Torres Strait Islander communities have been able to develop practical knowledge concerning the ethical conduct of research. In addition, bodies such as the Australian Institute of Aboriginal and Torres Strait Islander Studies (AIATSIS 2011) and the National Health and Medical Research Centre (NHMRC 2003) have made available guidelines which were adopted for this study.

Drawing on these guidelines, and in conjunction with feedback from internal stakeholders, we developed each stage of the research process in collaboration, namely; entry and contacting, informed consent, data collection, analysis and report writing and dissemination. The research team made sure that all practices were in line with research considerations by providing upfront detailed explanation and clarifications and also ensuring informed consent was freely granted prior to the formal commencement of each session. In line with our PAR approach these aspects were also agreed on collaboratively with our local partner researchers.

5.5 Methodology

5.5.1 Participatory Action Research

PAR requires active collaboration with participants and shared ownership of the research process (Burnes 2004; Jenks 1970; Miller et al. 2015). Philosophically, PAR is characterised by principles of empowerment, mutual ownership of research, the assumption that research leads to improvement, ongoing development of knowledge that integrates local perspectives, and a focus on solving practical, relevant issues. Highlighting its practical orientation, PAR has been defined as research that is conducted by ordinary people in collaboration with external researchers to explore questions and issues in daily life (Dickson and Green 2001; Holter and Schwartz-Barcott 1993; Masters 1995; McTaggart 1991; Miller et al. 2015). Recent work has demonstrated the value of PAR in creating collaborative partnerships with vulnerable and disadvantaged groups when working in areas such as pandemic influenza (Miller et al. 2015). Within PAR, the level of collaboration between researchers and local people can vary. A collaborative PAR strategy recognises the value of local perspectives and allows researchers to initiate change effectively based on pre-existing knowledge and expertise. Gradual transfer of power to local people (i.e., a collegiate approach; Cornwall and Jewkes 1995) may increase perceived ownership and commitment to sustaining the desired actions or changes that arise from research.

A typical PAR process is iterative consisting of cyclic repetitions of planning, action, observation and reflection (Burnes 2004; Fine and Torre 2014; McTaggart 1991). Others have described PAR as 'spiralled', in that knowledge and understanding—following reflection on data—informs the development of further research strategies, which in turn produces action. The adoption of this methodology is advantageous because it provides methodological flexibility in response to local needs and perspectives (Checkland and Howell 1998; Dickens and Watkins 1999; Fine 2013). Feeding back information to stakeholders at each 'spiral' ensures that the process is appropriate and may double as an intervention unto itself by raising awareness of issues and provoking local reflection (Dickens and Watkins 1999).

The Research Team A multi-disciplinary team was formed to conduct this consultative research. Participants were selected based on their areas of expertise and skills. Specifically, the primary team consisted of the Director of Research, the Director of Virtual Services, the Director of Aboriginal and Torres Strait Islander Programs and the Research Officer. Raw data were analysed by the Director of Research and Research Officer, with clarification and interpretative input from the two other team members.

5.5.2 *Participants*

Internal RAQ workers and community representatives participated in the research process. During the initial setup phase, the research team liaised with local community workers (Indigenous Service Delivery Advisors) to facilitate logistical operations and generate interest within the community. In addition, the Director of Aboriginal and Torres Strait Islander Programs and two Indigenous staff were linked in remotely (via video-conferencing) to each session to stimulate discussion and build rapport.

From a position of cultural respect and privacy, the demographic information of the participants will not be published. Each site included a mixture of RAQ staff and external parties. Leveraging off local knowledge, the local staff decided who the most appropriate community members would be to invite to participate. In one location (Thursday Island) all the community leaders were involved in the process, in other locations there was a smaller, but still significant, community leadership presence. The number of participants ranged between groups; Ipswich was the smallest group with five participants (including one community member), whereas Thursday Island was the largest, with nine participants (including seven community members). A wide consultative process ensured that, where possible, a diverse range of professional and cultural backgrounds were represented.

5.6 Method

The focus group technique is becoming increasingly popular across a range of disciplines as a method of conducting research. In particular, focus groups are often employed in cross-cultural research where literacy or accessibility may reduce the appropriateness of quantitative methods (Fine 2013; Fine and Torre 2014; Halcomb et al. 2007). Scholars have successfully conducted focus groups with culturally diverse participants including Aboriginal and Torres Strait Islander people (Halcomb et al. 2007; Miller et al. 2015) allowing for the expression of individual and community attitudes and values. This approach may also motivate action through the discussion of problems and potential solutions (Willis et al. 2005). In adapting the focus group format to suit an Aboriginal research context, Willis et al. (2005) provided two recommendations; the importance developing a background understanding of the problem through community consultation and allowing for flexibility in the agenda and questioning process.

The research team developed focus group questions that corresponded to each identified area of technology acceptance; specifically:

1. Design: Maximising the user experience through features (aesthetic, usability) of the system interface
2. Implementation: Ensuring uptake of technologies through effective marketing and promotion, and implementation success through the development and maintenance of collaborative relationships with community stakeholders
3. Service delivery: Accounting for protocols and preferences through the development of culturally appropriate service delivery models

Further, the research team developed a realistic scenario that guided the demonstration of the OFDR system. Scenarios are commonly used in focus group research to provide participants with a shared context against which evaluations and recommendations can be made (Fine 2013; Miller et al. 2015; Sato and Salvador 1999). Historically statistics suggested that Aboriginal and Torres Strait Islander people had less experience with computer technology (ACMA 2008). This access gap between Indigenous and non-Indigenous people appears to be reducing in more recently published statistics (ABS 2012). With this in mind we leveraged staged demonstrations to encourage participation and engagement in each session.

The scenario consisted of a mock intake session followed by a significantly abridged family dispute resolution session. At least one Aboriginal or Torres Strait Islander member of staff was remotely linked into each session to participate in group discussions. A member of the research team acted in the role of the OFDR practitioner (remotely linked in), and two facilitators answered questions and prompted discussions.

Adopting a flexible approach (Willis et al. 2005), each focus group followed a similar structure and process that was interspersed with opportunities to contribute freely. Time was spent introducing the project and objectives, followed by round-table introductions. Each participant provided background information, such as their name, cultural heritage and area(s) of work, as mentioned above to ensure anonymity these details are omitted. Next, the research team demonstrated the use of the technology using a scripted scenario. Specifically, the demonstration consisted of the following distinct sections:

- Initial welcoming of client and coaching regarding the process of the online appointment (demonstrating the use of the shared presentation feature)
- Disclosure of required information to clients about the mediation process using video and voice communication (demonstrating the document sharing and video-conferencing features)
- Abridged intake questioning process, including discussion of mediation topics (demonstrating electronic form completion and collaborative document creation feature)
- Mock referral of the client to legal services using online resources (demonstrating screen-sharing capabilities)
- Simulation of the initial stages of a mediation (demonstrating the use of 'break-out' or private rooms and three-way use of video and voice communication)
- Simulated discussion of agenda items and possible solutions (demonstrating collaborative document creation)
- Use of visual metaphors as a technique to encourage a child focussed perspective during mediation discussions (demonstrating the shared whiteboard and touch-screen drawing features)

A pause was inserted following each section of the demonstration, which allowed discussions to emerge unimpeded. Further, we adopted the 'funnelled' approach to focus group questioning (Beyea and Nicoll 2000; Halcomb et al. 2007; Morgan 1997) meaning our discussions were facilitated to openly encourage disclosure and engagement. Specific questioning was introduced in successive stages of the demonstration to ensure all areas of interest were covered. Participants were also provided with an opportunity to make concluding remarks or suggestions.

In line with PAR processes, the research team participated in a reflective process following each focus group session (Dickson and Green 2001). Reflections were completed independently by each team member in relation to elements done well, areas for improvement and recommendations. Responses to reflective questions were generated within the following areas and used to inform subsequent focus group iterations:

- Personal performance
- Logistics/equipment/general organisation
- Session structure
- Facilitation
- Open-ended comments

Demonstrating the cyclic and iterative process of PAR, the feedback and reflections from each session were used to plan the subsequent focus group. The research team collaborated in this planning process using verbal discussions that referenced and integrated the content from individual reflections. Consequently, the format and facilitation of the final focus group benefited from two previous action research iterations. At the conclusion of the initial consultative process, facilitators' reflections were collated and subjected to qualitative analysis—emerging themes were used to facilitate organisational and individual learning.

Data Collection Procedures Preferably, qualitative analysis is performed on transcribed interviews or focus groups (Creswell 2009). This procedure ensures that the richness of the original context and meaning are preserved during the coding process. With the consent of the focus group participants, each session was video-recorded. Two researchers then played back each session and manually transcribed each line of conversation into electronic documents. Ambiguities were clarified using session notes recorded by the researchers.

Data Analysis Procedures The analysis of qualitative data consists of several distinct steps. Typically, qualitative analysis is a 'sense-making' process whereby data are initially prepared, coded, themed and then verified through discussion and consultation (Creswell 2009). The aim of qualitative research is to move from a purely descriptive representation of data to increasing levels of abstraction (Creswell 2007, 2009).

During the coding process, researchers may benefit from the adoption of a systematic approach (Saldana 2009). Our strategy for the analysis consisted of three 'passes' over the data. We began with a combination of initial and in-vivo coding to summarise the body of text. Second, codes were revised and reorganised into more meaningful higher-order categories. Third, categories were grouped together to form overarching themes.

Verification Validity and reliability are important issues to address during qualitative research (Creswell and Miller 2000; Darawsheh 2014; Gibbs 2007). In a qualitative context, validity refers to the data-checking procedures employed by the researcher to ensure the findings are accurate; reliability relates to the adoption of a consistent approach to data collection across participants and settings (Gibbs 2007).

Within this study, we employed a number of procedures to ensure adequate validity and reliability of the results:

1. Review of video-taped sessions
2. Engaging in individual reflection following each session, which informed future iterations and research analysis
3. Following a scripted demonstration process across groups
4. Seeking contribution and verification of data interpretation from local workers and internal stakeholders
5. Transcribing all notes, and video recordings verbatim
6. Coding by two researchers, discrepancies in codes and themes were resolved through discussion.

Consequently, we are confident that the data collection and analysis procedures retained integrity.

5.7 Results

We analysed both the content of the focus group discussions and the reflections of the facilitators. Focus group discussions were grouped into nine overarching content domains; community implementation, awareness of cultural diversity, the *digital divide*, social and cultural context, broad applications, service engagement and promotion, clinical skill-set, visual and auditory design and geographical location. Reflective data were organised into eight overarching themes; an 'easy' process, *setting up the basics*, prior testing, research integrity, session effectiveness, practical constraints, community consultation and emerging clarity. For brevity, we present summarised findings from each of these themes and briefly explore each with reference to exemplary participant statements. Models of themes are presented below.

5.7.1 Focus Group Content

Community Implementation OFDR should be implemented at the community level, via a gradual, deliberate process and in collaboration with existing services. Moreover, participants suggested a range of suitable community settings (e.g., libraries, community centres, major services, RAQ offices). Within regional and remote communities, home environments are likely to be inappropriate for OFDR due to a perceived inability to satisfy privacy requirements ("the stuff like private environment—you aren't going to get that"). A community-based location was strongly recommended ("because people are more likely to come there [community locations], to get away from the family").

Awareness of Cultural Diversity Cultural diversity must be acknowledged and respected throughout any implementation process; diversity not only between non-Indigenous and Indigenous peoples, but also diversity between and within cultures, groups/communities and individuals ("each town is different, and within that town there is diversity as well. Even within Aboriginal and Torres Strait Islanders, there is diversity, the different island groups"). Building local knowledge by engaging internal workers and community networks will assist providers to contextualise their service offerings and develop awareness of relevant cultural and community protocols.

The Digital Divide Inequity in technological access between Indigenous and non-Indigenous, urban and regional/remote, represents the biggest challenge to the implementation of OFDR ("access to computers is going to be the biggest issue"). Technology, such as computer and cell phones, was still largely a novel phenomenon to many Aboriginal and Torres Strait Islander community participants, which produced excitement ("they are just excited about being on a computer, because it's exciting, because it's something new and out there") and also intimidation ("we understand that, but because it's remote, this is scary").

Social and Cultural Context Technology implementations must consider the social and cultural context into which they are entering—for many remote communities, basic needs such as food and shelter are priorities ("the priority is always feed your family, and a roof over your head"). Technology needs to be flexible and affordable to reduce the impact on families and should aim to meet some of these basic needs to maximize uptake ("if there's a cost involve too, if it comes across—how much is it?"). Additional concerns such as numeracy, literacy, and mental and physical health are commonplace within these communities, this too must be considered when designing services and systems.

Broad Applications Participants could envisage a broad range of applications for the OFDR system—centring on the use of the system for communicative purposes ("using this system will be good as we are face to face, bring us together"). Specific applications raised by participants included contact between family members, either supervised parent/child contact or in cases of estrangement due to distance, family violence, court matters or incarceration. Other uses included education, professional networking and supervision. The participants also felt that the system could be used to encourage counselling and other relevant service referrals among family members ("women in shelters are embarrassed and everyone sees them go to mental health, this could help those women by bringing service to them and also allowing them to encourage their men to go for counselling").

Service Engagement and Promotion Attention must be paid to respectfully engaging and promoting the OFDR system within communities if the service is to be seen to be acceptable, appropriate and useful by potential consumers. Perceptions of the service are influenced by cultural, community and individual preferences. New services should be seen to be worthy of trust ("it comes down to making the point that it is a confidential service, and your information is not going to be out in the community") and demonstrate a genuine desire to understand and help clients ("if we can try to meet those needs to the best of our ability, I think that the client is going to know that their needs have been put first"). In addition, provisions should be made to facilitate easy transitions between services ("sometimes it probably feels like shopping around for the right doctor").

Clinical Skill-set An OFDR service must empower practitioners with a particular clinical practice skill set and an appropriate service delivery model if it is to be perceived as culturally-appropriate. The service must be flexible, be mindful of client preferences, anticipate reactions to technical hitches and adequately support clients prior to, and throughout the process. Of note, the importance of support people emerged as a particularly strong theme ("my only worry is ensuring that people participating in such disputes have a support person who is really aware of what they are going through"); specifically, in terms of emotional, cultural, technical, legal and linguistically appropriate support. In addition, participants recommended that clients should be provided with adequate preparation prior to their first session ("but obviously, there is a lot of preparation needed"). This preparation should provide adequate information of both technical and procedural aspects of their participation in the service.

Visual and Auditory Design Regarding system design, it is important to acknowledge that Aboriginal and Torres Strait Islander culture emphasizes the role of both visual ("our people are very visual too") and auditory ("our language is varied, our language is an oral language") media. The attention of these visual and auditory peoples must be captured in order to engage them ("to capture their attention for a start") through the richness and aesthetic appeal of media. For example, participants felt it was important to "instil the culture" into the media through the use of appropriate cultural artwork, photography, iconography and colour schemes. While participants were attracted by the idea of cultural adaption and localisation ("I would want to see something different, like a more contemporary design"), there was an acknowledgement that this may be perceived differently by individuals and there may be a need to compromise between localisation and generic designing. Specifically, some individuals may find politically-influenced design (e.g., use of the Aboriginal flag) as contentious. Regardless, design that embraces a mixture of visual and auditory media is vital to ensure that a positive first impression is connoted to clients ("always get it right the first time").

Geographical Location The needs and preferences of Aboriginal and Torres Strait Islander clients may vary as a function of their geographical location. The need for services and the availability of services and resources (such as the required technology) differ depending on the geographic are of implementation. Participants discussed the importance of the level of perceived equity in service provision between urban and remote locations ("I think the main thing that is coming across, is that people in remote or regional areas are going to access quality services just as people who live 5 minutes away from a branch would").

5.7.2 Reflective Content

An 'Easy' Process The OFDR community consultations were assisted greatly by the facilitation of an 'easy' process. This ease was largely due to the level of engagement of the participants ("equal control of the process between participants and facilitators; at times, discussions were very much participant led"). The staged demonstration approach, which allowed the facilitators to provide a structured showcase of the OFDR system with a minimal impact on the flow of discussions, also contributed to the perceived 'ease'. The relatively structured approach ensured consistency between groups while allowing sufficient flexibility to enable free flow of ideas from participants ("yet the session was sufficiently fluid for the group to discuss different issues as they were raised").

Setting Up the Basics The theme 'setting up the basics' refers to the establishment of a positive and welcoming environment to ensure that participants feel comfortable engaging in discussions. In particular, observing cultural protocol and formalities, establishing rapport and trust and remaining mindful of the 'comings and goings' of participants in community settings is vital for a successful consultative process. Facilitators also reflected that more opportunities for participant contributions could have been valuable; specifically, discussions ("I found myself speaking more") and interaction with technology ("we should encourage them to come up and try it").

Prior Testing Given the high reliance on technology throughout the consultative process, better testing procedures could have enabled the project team to prepare for unexpected challenges. Whereas the majority of technology functioned well, assumptions were made relating to the capacity of the telephone handsets to capture group discussions ("we made an assumption about the phone working").

Research Integrity Across multiple sessions, it was important to maintain the integrity of the action research project. Several challenges presented themselves during the consultative process, including session consistency, ethical considerations and questioning procedures. Whereas improvements could have been made to the standardisation of the demonstration ("a video could be used in the future to ensure a standardised stimulus across groups"), the facilitators agreed sufficient consistency was maintained ("relatively consistent between groups"). In addition, researchers must remain mindful of spontaneous ethical dilemmas that may arise ("on reflection I was concerned that one of the participants was clearly uncomfortable to be filmed and yet signed the consent form"). Subsequent groups noted that the concern may not have been ethically problematic but that Aboriginal and Torres Strait Islander peoples are often 'camera shy' and embarrassed to see themselves on film. This has clear implications for the use of video streaming technology that need to be considered in the design stages.

Session Effectiveness The sessions were considered to be effective, with aspects of the research design including methods of participant contribution (written and verbal), group composition and the perceived credibility of facilitators. Group diversity and inclusion of respected members of the community ("the presence of elders and other familiar/respected members of the community seems to be a vital component of engagement") as well as RAQ Indigenous workers ("ensure RAQ staff are present to support the facilitators and provide trust-transfer") were particularly effective at maximising the value of each consultation.

Practical Constraints The research team contended with a number of practical constraints, which we believe impacted minimally on the overall effectiveness of the sessions. Specifically, short timeframes to organise each consultation, the cost of travelling to remote communities and unexpected location issues ("space at the FRC was very tight") may have impacted the consultations. Anticipating such practical issues in subsequent stages may further reduce any impact.

Principles for Community Engagement The consultative process experienced by the OFDR team surfaced a number of strategies that contributed to its success. These strategies included principles for engaging communities, leveraging local staff and the importance of forming long-term partnerships with communities. In particular, strong and consistent communication with internal stakeholders was, at times, difficult to maintain. At times it was necessary to 'reconnect' staff to the project to ensure continued support. Local workers were instrumental in setting up each session. Given the research team's distance from clients and lack of familiarity with these communities, the assistance of the RAQ employees in the consultation process was invaluable ("local Aboriginal and Torres Strait Islander support workers and venue manager were instrumental in this process"). Critically, we believe that from these meetings, partnerships began to be formed which could be developed with follow-up visits and involvement in research analysis ("And then go back to the communities and give them feedback about the response at the conference, that would be helpful, and they might even have more feedback for us and we can build that into the research"). Indeed, the Thursday Island community were so engaged with the technology that an interim committee was formed to assist the research team with future steps in the project.

Emerging Clarity Over the course of four demonstration sessions, the facilitators indicated that clarity emerged surrounding their roles, the purpose of the sessions, level of preparation required and the involvement of remote users. On reflection, the facilitators indicated that additional preparation, in the form of rehearsals and increasing local cultural knowledge would have been useful ("I had not prepared sufficiently in regards to researching the area that we were visiting"). While some preparation was planned, not all researchers were able to attend due to conflicting schedules. As the sessions were repeated with the benefit of reflection between sessions, any short comings in this area in the early stages were quickly addressed ("we were now well familiar with the demonstration and our roles").

5.8 Discussion

Overall, our research produced fruitful preliminary results in relation to the design, implementation and promotion of a new online mediation service within Aboriginal and Torres Strait Islander communities. Results indicated that the participating communities were ready and enthused by the concept of online service delivery, although there were some concerns regarding cultural relevance, confidentiality, useability and accessibility. In seeking input at the early stages of OFDR design and developing an understanding of the barriers as perceived by the consumers, these concerns can more readily be overcome in subsequent development and roll out.

With modification and ongoing consultation with community reference groups, the OFDR system can be contextualised and adapted to suit local needs, although given the costs involved of system design full localisation may not be feasible and some compromise may be required (Reinecke and Bernstein 2013). Cost control will necessarily be a key component of the service, so the challenge is always to ensure what funds are available are directed for maximum benefit. Future consultations should focus on greater participant involvement with the technology to closely evaluate the usability and cultural-appropriateness of actioned system modifications and service delivery procedures. Through ongoing involvement from co-researchers, the end design should meet community expectations and requirements, while providing high quality service.

Our PAR methodology, which focussed on principles of collaboration, engagement, mutual ownership and reflective iteration, resulted in a rigorous research procedure that was responsive to the community context. In addition, a structured, yet free flowing and easy focus group process ensured that participant engagement and technological understanding was maximised. Moreover, a realistic simulation of OFDR services helped to provide context to an audience that was for the most part, relatively unfamiliar with both mediation process and online technologies.

Local workers and the involvement of community members were key to logistical organisation and group engagement and effectiveness of the consultation. Extensive, regular and personal communication with internal stakeholders proved to be valuable in maintaining project enthusiasm. Where communication issues did occur, reconnecting with workers quickly reinvigorated support and clarified expectations.

Many practical suggestions were proposed by focus group participants in relation to design, service engagement, community implementation and clinical practice. Of note, were the observed parallels among our initial review of the literature around cultural considerations and the suggestions raised by participants. Specifically, the importance of a flexible process (Davies 2007; Miller et al. 2015; Spangaro et al. 2016), inclusion of support people for consumers (Matthews and Burton 2013; McLoughlin and Oliver 2000), involvement of Elders and community members (Crawford and Thwaites 2012; Vindigni et al. 2004), localised system design (Butchmann 2000; Dyson 2003; McCann et al. 2000; McLoughlin and Oliver 2000; Reinecke and Bernstein 2013), social/economic context (ABS 2012; Bauman and Pope 2009; Commonwealth of Australia 2017; Hattotuwa and Conley Tyler 2005), community consultation (Crawford and Thwaites 2012; Eagles et al. 2005; Moran et al. 2009; Turner 2017) and differences in gender roles and preferences (Bauman and Pope 2009; Spangaro et al. 2016). This convergence is reassuring and should inspire confidence in the themes presented here.

Given the positive reception we are confident that a design that considers culturally influenced preferences and practical concerns (such as the service being provided at a facility and not the consumers' home) will be well received in these communities. FDR is an important service for all Australians, however as it can be less adversarial than litigation and take into account more aspects of the family and community, it is especially well culturally-suited to Aboriginal and Torres Strait Island peoples. Given the vast distances between inhabited areas in much of Australia, an OFDR system will be able to provide high quality service to remote areas that would otherwise be underserved in terms of quality, or have infrequent access from a travelling professional.

5.8.1 Strengths

Analysis of the facilitators' reflective journals and review of the research methodology revealed several strengths of the current study. While our process can be considered emergent, it is nevertheless a strong and well considered approach that achieved acceptable validity and reliability through considered research design. Leveraging the resources of multiple internal stakeholders and Aboriginal and Torres Strait Islander workers ensured that the emerging themes and codes were interpreted accurately. These subject matter experts were available to clarify the comments made by participants and provided additional context to the research team during the data analysis process. This additional context meant that the data was richer and provided a more holistic view of the concerns and expectations of the potential consumers. In this way these participants were certainly co-researchers, vital for conducting PAR with Indigenous communities (Miller et al. 2015). This wide-reaching consultation process also highlighted the benefits of both community and local worker involvement. Facilitators observed that engagement and rapport were vastly improved when Indigenous workers were able to attend and participate in the sessions (even by remote video linkup). Scaffolding off existing relationships to form new and ongoing partnerships is vital for engagement. These partnerships must be developed over time to facilitate trust and to avoid the perception of a paternalistic approach (Wilson 2016).

Our methodology highlighted the importance of integrating reflective learnings into each session. Over time, clarity around roles, structure and facilitation emerged through active consideration of session content. Video-taping each focus group added considerably to the learning that occurred for the facilitators and provided additional (visual) data to include in the analysis process. Further input from participants with regards their level of comfort being videotaped should be considered in future and weighed against the advantages of the use of video recordings. Options for OFDR service delivery that do not include video, such as audio only, should also be considered in light of these concerns.

Finally, an extensive background literature review together with prior experience of the first author with PAR methodology and implementation (Wilson-Evered et al. 2001), the engagement of communities by our Aboriginal leader as well as the knowledge and technical expertise of our other team members were all strengths of the approach. Specifically, the integration of previous research recommendations and collated principles combined with grounded multidisciplinary and culturally diverse knowledge and expertise proved to be a valuable source of guidance in the development of our approach for this study.

5.8.2 Limitations

Practical constraints introduced limitations to this study. Community participation was limited at Townsville and Ipswich due to the challenges of remote organisation and lack of time. Short notice restricted the availability of local representatives. In addition, better communication between the research team and the local venue leader may have avoided the issue of the Townsville session date coinciding with a local community event. Staff indicated that this scheduling clash may have prevented additional participants from attending. Additional time to build relationships and better understand the local environment may avoid these issues in future.

While the inclusion of local workers was vital for organisation and rapport building, their inclusion in the focus groups may have influenced the participant responses. To address this input from these workers could be obtained through specific demonstrations so as to ensure the other participants were not influenced. Although it could also be possible that their involvement in session allowed the participants to feel more at ease and able to be open and honest. Future researchers will need to weigh up the possible advantages and disadvantages of each approach, a case by case decision would be most appropriate.

5.8.3 Future Research

The research team plans to return to these communities in the near future. Ongoing partnerships are to be maintained through regular communication and consultation to ensure that these relationships remain strong over time (Miller et al. 2015). At the time of the presentations there were high levels of enthusiasm, however this has waned over time and researchers should expect to devote time for relationship building prior to any data collection (Wilson 2016). Ethically, RAQ is obliged to ensure that these communities receive benefits from research through knowledge-sharing and empowerment strategies (AIATSIS 2011; NHMRC 2003). This represents an ongoing challenge for researchers who are often funded only for the period of project planning, data collection, analysis and presentation. Future research should consider including additional time to develop community partnerships and share findings into their initial grant applications (Crawford and Thwaites 2012; Matthews and Burton 2013).

Future research is recommended in the area of human-computer interaction for Aboriginal and Torres Strait Islander peoples. In particular, the influence of system interface design on overall user experience in an Indigenous context has been neglected to date. Arguably, if technology based services are to be implemented successfully with Aboriginal and Torres Strait Islander communities, basic challenges to uptake such as system usability need to be addressed from a cross-cultural perspective. From the preliminary research conducted here, continuing to ignore the role of culture in system design is likely to perpetuate inequity and disadvantage as consumers may missed out on the benefits of the service if not appropriately tailored.

Given the emerging themes relating to low service awareness and urgent needs in remote and regional communities, providers need to demonstrate to funding bodies that meaningful work can be performed. Noting the benefits of working holistically with Aboriginal and Torres Strait Islander people (Reeve and Bradford 2014), these services would ideally be linked with collaboration among the service providers with the best outcome for consumers the end goal. Given the challenges faced by not-for-profit organisations conducting research that evidences funding applications, networking, knowledge-sharing and inter-agency learning are recommended to address resource shortfall (Carman and Fredericks 2010).

Finally, we believe the outcomes of this study could inform guidelines to shape future consultations and service development. This should include an evaluative component to assess the degree to which services address the needs of Aboriginal and Torres Strait Islander people in a cultural appropriate, collaborative way.

References

Australian Bureau of Statistics (2012) Census of population and housing: characteristics of Aboriginal and Torres Strait Islander Australians. http://www.abs.gov.au/AUSSTATS/abs@.nsf/mediareleasesbyReleaseDate/CD6742DF2845507CCA258236000C3242?OpenDocument

Australian Bureau of Statistics (ABS) (2002) National Aboriginal and Torres Strait Islander Social Survey. ABS, Canberra

Australian Communications and Media Authority (ACMA) (2008) Telecommunications in remote Indigenous communities. https://www.acma.gov.au/theACMA/telecommunications-in-remote-indigenous-communities

Australian Institute of Aboriginal and Torres Strait Islander Studies (AIATSIS) (2011) Guidelines for ethical research in Australian indigenous studies. https://aiatsis.gov.au/research/ethical-research/guidelines-ethical-research-australian-indigenous-studies

Bauman T, Pope J (2009) Solid work you mob are doing: case studies in Indigenous dispute resolution and conflict management in Australia. Commonwealth of Australia, Canberra

Beyea S, Nicoll L (2000) Methods to conduct focus groups and the moderator's role. AORN J 71:1067–1068

Branas J, Gooda M (2006) Putting the users of research in the driver's seat: the Cooperative Research Centre for Aboriginal Health's new approach to research development. Aust Aboriginal Stud 2:27–35

Burnes B (2004) Kurt Lewin and the planned approach to change: a re-appraisal. J Manag Stud 4:976–1002

Butchmann L (2000) Digital songlines: the use of modern communication by an Aboriginal community in remote Australia. Prometheus 18:59–74

Carman J, Fredericks K (2010) Evaluation capacity and nonprofit organizations: is the glass half-empty or half-full? Am J Eval 31:84–104

Checkland P, Howell S (1998) Information, systems and information systems: making sense of the field. Wiley, Chichester

Commonwealth of Australia (2017) Closing the gap. https://www.pmc.gov.au/indigenous-affairs/closing-gap

Conroy S (2010) Second release sites announced for NBN rollout. 10 July. https://www.if.com.au/second-release-sites-announced-for-nbn-rollout/

Cornwall A, Jewkes R (1995) What is participatory research. Soc Sci Med 41:1667–1676

Crawford W, Thwaites R (2012) Two way learning and culturally appropriate mediation training in remote communities. Indigenous Law Bull 8:24–27

Creswell W (2007) Qualitative inquiry and research design: choosing among five approaches. Sage Publications, London

Creswell W (2009) Research design: qualitative, quantitative and mixed methods approaches. Sage Publications, London

Creswell W, Miller D (2000) Determining validity in qualitative inquiry. Theory Pract 39:124–130

Cullen R (2001) Addressing the digital divide. Online Inf Rev 25:311–320

Daly A (2006) Bridging the digital divide: the role of community online access centres in Indigenous communities. Demetrius. http://dspace.anu.edu.au/handle/1885/43177

Darawsheh W (2014) Reflexivity in research: promoting rigour, reliability and validity in qualitative research. Int J Ther Rehabil 21:560–568

Davies J (2007) 'Walking together, working together': aboriginal research partnerships. Desert Knowledge Cooperative Research Centre, Alice Springs

Demeester M (1999) Cultural aspects of information technology implementation. Int J Med Inform 6:25–41

Dickens L, Watkins K (1999) Action research: rethinking Lewin. Manag Learn 30:127–140

Dickson G, Green K (2001) The external researcher in participatory action research. Educ Action Res 9:243–260

Dyson L (2002) Design for a culturally affirming Indigenous computer literacy course. Paper presented at ASCILITE 2002, UNITEC Institute of Technology, Auckland, 8–11 December 2002

Dyson L (2003) Indigenous Australians in the information age: exploring issues of neutrality in information technology. In: Ciborra C, Mercurio R, De Marco M, Martinez M, Carignani A (eds) New paradigms in organizations, markets and society: Proceedings of the 11th European Conference on Information System, Naples, Italy, 19–21 June 2003

Eades S (2000) Reconciliation, social equity and Indigenous health: a call for symbolic and material change. Aborig Isl Health Work J 24:3–4

Eagles D, Woodward P, Pope M (2005) Indigenous learners in the digital age: recognising skills and knowledge. Paper presented at The 8th Annual AVETRA Conference, Brisbane, Australia, 13–15 April 2005

Faulkner J (2015) Our own Hurricane Katrina': aboriginal disadvantage and Australian national identity. Natl Ident 17:117–135

Fine M (2013) Echoes of Bedford: a 20-year social psychology memoir on participatory action research hatched behind bars. Am Psychol 68:687–698

Fine TL (2014) Theories of probability: an examination of foundations. Academic Press

Fine M, Torre ME (2014) Re-membering exclusions: participatory action research in public institutions. Qual Res Psychol 1:15–37

Frandsen-Thorlacius O, Hornbæk K, Hertzem M, Clemmensen T (2009) Non-universal usability? A survey of how usability is understood by Chinese and Danish users. Paper presented at the SIGCHI Conference on Human Factors in Computing Systems, Boston, USA, 4–9 April 200

Gibbs G (2007) Analysing qualitative data. Sage Publications, London

Halcomb E, Gholizadeh L, DiGiacomo M, Phillips J, Davidson P (2007) Literature review: considerations in undertaking focus group research with culturally and linguistically diverse groups. J Clin Nurs 16:1000–1011

Hattotuwa S, Conley Tyler M (2005) An Asian perspective on online mediation. Asia J Mediation 1:13–37

Henry J, Dunbar T, Arnott A, Scrimgeour M, Murakami-Gold L (2004) Indigenous research reform agenda: a review of the literature. Links Monograph Series 5, CRCATH, Darwin, Australia

Holter I, Schwartz-Barcott D (1993) Action research: what is it? How has it been used and how can it be used in nursing? J Adv Nurs 18:298–304

Humphrey K (2001) Dirty questions: Indigenous health and 'Western research'. Aust N Z J Public Health 25:197–202

Hunter E (2003) Staying tuned to developments in Indigenous health: reflections on a decade of change. Aust Psychiatry 11:418–423

Jagne J, Smith-Atakan A (2006) Cross-cultural interface design strategy. Comput Sci 5:299–305

Jenks R (1970) An action-research approach to organizational change. J Appl Behav Sci 6:131–150

Khaddam I, Vanderdonckt J (2014) Towards a culture-adaptable user interface architecture. Revista Română de Interacțiune Om-Calculator 7:161–194

Markus HR, Kitayama S (1991) Culture and self: implication for cognition, emotion and motivation. Psychol Rev 98:224–253

Masters J (1995) The history of action research. In: Hughes I (ed) Action research electronic reader. The University of Sydney. http://www.aral.com.au/arow/rmasters.html

Matthews G, Burton J (2013) Promising practice in intensive family support for Aboriginal and Torres Strait Islander families. Dev Pract 34:56–65

McCann S, Greenleaf G, Chung P, Austin D (2000) Reconciliation online: reflections and possibilities. UTS Law Rev 2:139–152

McIntyre J (2003) Yeperenye dreaming in conceptual, geographical, and cyberspace: a participatory action research approach to address local governance within an Australian Indigenous housing association. Syst Pract Action Res 16:309–338

McLoughlin C, Oliver R (2000) Designing learning environments for cultural inclusivity: a case study of Indigenous online learning at tertiary level. Aust J Educ Technol 16:58–72

McTaggart R (1991) Principles for participatory action research. Educ Q 41:168–187

Miller A, Massey PD, Judd J, Kelly J, Durrhein DN, Clough AR, Speare R, Saggers S (2015) Using a participatory action research framework to listen to Aboriginal and Torres Strait Islander people in Australia about pandemic influenza. Rural Remote Health 15:2923–2932

Moran M, Anda M, Kennedy A, Long S, McFallan S, McGrath N, Memmott P, Mulgan R, Stanley O, Sullivan P, Tedmanson D, Wright A, Young M (2009) Desert services that work: year one research report. Desert Knowledge Cooperative Research Centre, Alice Springs

Morgan D (1997) Focus groups as qualitative research, 2nd edn. Sage Publications, Thousand Oaks

National Health and Medical Research Centre (NHMRC) (2003) Values and ethics - guidelines for ethical conduct in Aboriginal and Torres Strait Islander health research. https://nhmrc.gov.au/about-us/publications/values-and-ethics-guidelines-ethical-conduct-aboriginal-and-torres-strait-islander-health-research

Noiwan J, Norcio A (2006) Cultural differences on attention and perceived usability: investigating color combination of animated graphics. Int J Hum Comput Stud 64:103–122

Olson G, Olson J (2003) Human-computer interaction: psychological aspects of the human use of computing. Annu Rev Psychol 54:491–516

Onibere E, Morgan S, Busang E, Mpoeleng D (2001) Human-Computer interface design issues for a multi-cultural and multi-lingual English speaking country – Botswana. Interact Comput 13:497–512

Parmaxi A, Zaphiris P (2016) Computer-mediated communication in computer-assisted language learning: implications for culture-centered design. Univ Access Inf Soc 15:169–177

Petrie N, Kruger L (2014) Child protection matters in the Northern Territory. Altern Law J 39:104–109

Radoll P (2014) Cyber-safety and Indigenous youth. Indigenous Law Bull 8:11–14

Rainey D (2012) ODR and culture. In: Abdel Wahab MS, Katsh E, Rainey D (eds) Online dispute resolution: theory and practice. Eleven International Publishing, The Hague, pp 185–201

Rao S (2004) The cultural vacuum in online dispute resolution. Paper presented at the Third Annual Forum on Online Dispute Resolution

Reeve R, Bradford W (2014) Aboriginal disadvantage in major cities of New South Wales: evidence for holistic policy approaches. Aust Econ Rev 47:199–217

Reinecke K, Bernstein A (2013) Knowing what a user likes: a design science approach to interfaces that automatically adapt to culture. MIS Q 37:427–453

Rigney L (2006) Indigenous research and Aboriginal Australia. In: Kunnie J, Goduka N (eds) Indigenous people's wisdom and power: affirming our knowledge through narratives. Ashgate Publishing, Surrey, pp 34–48

Saldana J (2009) The coding manual for qualitative research. Sage Publications, London

Sato S, Salvador T (1999) Playacting and focus troupes: theatre techniques for creating quick, intense, immersive and engaging focus group sessions. Interactions Sept/Oct:35–41

Spangaro J, Herring S, Koziol-Mclain J, Rutherford A, Frail M, Zwi AB (2016) They aren't really black fellas but they are easy to talk to': factors which influence Australian Aboriginal women's decision to disclose intimate partner violence during pregnancy. Midwifery 41:79–88

Thomson M (2011) Alternative modes of delivery for family dispute resolution: the Telephone Dispute Resolution Service and the online FDR project. J Fam Stud 17:253–257

Tractinsky N (2000) A theoretical framework and empirical examination of the effects of foreign and translated interface language. Behav Inform Technol 19:1–14

Tsey K, Wilson A, Haswell-Elkins M, Whiteside M, McCalman J, Cadet-James Y, Wenitong M (2007) Empowerment-based research methods: a 10-year approach to enhancing Indigenous social and emotional wellbeing. Aust Psychiatry 16:S34–S38

Turner P (2017) Ten years of Close the Gap: why are we sicker, poorer and living shorter than the rest of Australia. https://www.sbs.com.au/nitv/article/2017/03/15/ten-years-close-gap-why-are-we-sicker-poorer-and-living-shorter-rest-australia

Varan D (1998) The cultural erosion metaphor and the transcultural impact of media systems. J Commun 48:58–85

Vindigni D, Parkinson L, Blunden S, Perkins J, Rivett D, Walker B (2004) Aboriginal health in Aboriginal hands: development, delivery and evaluation of a training programme for Aboriginal health workers to promote the musculoskeletal health of Indigenous people living in a rural community. Int Electron J Rural Remote Health Res 4:1–10

Willis E, Pearce M, Jenkin T (2005) Adapting focus group methods to fit Aboriginal community-based research. Qual Res J 5:112–123

Wilson L (2016) Closing the gap: leading innovation in Indigenous education. Independence 41:76–81

Wilson-Evered E, Härtel CE, Neale M (2001) A longitudinal study of work group innovation: the importance of transformational leadership and morale. In: Friedman LH, Goes J, Savage GT (eds) Advances in health care management. Emerald Group Publishing Limited, pp 315–340

Chapter 6
Concluding Thoughts

Abstract This book has presented the case for the value of integrating technologies into the family law arena particularly within Australian contexts but with clear implications for family dispute resolution (FDR) services worldwide. Online dispute resolution (ODR) has already experienced success across a wide range of other conflicts, with preliminary evidence in the growing field of online family dispute resolution (OFDR) showing favourable outcomes for separating parents. The research presented in this book supports arguments that OFDR increases access to quality FDR services which in turn facilitates child-centered decision-making. This chapter will summarise the lessons learned to-date to inform recommendations for future OFDR program design and improvement. Both ODR and OFDR are relatively young developments in Australia, so the potential of these advanced technologies and their capabilities is yet unknown. Continued rigorous research into existing and future OFDR programs will further improve the field and the outcomes for families, an endeavour that will take the collaboration of many different stakeholders and a commitment to ongoing learning and future-focused change.

6.1 Introduction

Throughout this book, evidence has been presented to advocate for the use of online technologies in supporting the delivery of family dispute services. Far from being simply a more convenient way of accessing services, the case for online technologies to complement current face-to-face methods of family dispute resolution (FDR) is robust. In Australia, online family dispute resolution (OFDR) is a growing field of interest within both public and private sectors, with legal and social environments considered hospitable to nurturing its advancement.

Namely, as was detailed in Chap. 1, the establishment of the Family Law Act in Australia in 1975 helped to set the scene for later innovation via the implementation of a specialist family court (Nicholson and Harrison 2000). In 2006, the Commonwealth government passed legislation to make FDR a mandatory prerequisite for most individuals, excluding those in extenuating circumstances. Not just designed to

E. Wilson-Evered, J. Zeleznikow, *Online Family Dispute Resolution*, Law, Governance and Technology Series 45,
https://doi.org/10.1007/978-3-030-64645-5_6

be a 'tick-box' exercise, separating parents were expected to make a genuine effort to resolve their disputes prior to court involvement, if necessary. To assist in the realization of these Family Law Reforms, the Australian government provided funding for 65 family relationship centres (FRCs) to operate across the nation. These centres facilitated free or heavily subsidised support to separating families by offering FDR services and information to reduce resource strain on the legal system and emotional strain on families (Parkinson 2013). Such a change from adversarial procedures was considered consistent with child-centred practices by keeping the child's wellbeing and interests at the foreground of any family dispute process. This new era of family support also acknowledged the continuation of the parenting relationship after separation had been finalized, thereby taking a longitudinal approach to support as opposed to seeing the dispute as an isolated event in time.

It has been proposed that online technologies can provide additional options for families in lieu of court intervention. Although the focus of this book has been dedicated to investigating the potential of online family dispute resolution (OFDR) capabilities, Chaps. 2 and 3 identified some of the varying family services that can be enhanced through technological solutions. For instance, counselling services can be delivered in online formats (Augar and Zeleznikow 2014; Knight and Hunter 2013), apps have been developed to assist in co-parenting collaboration and communication (e.g., *mymob, Our Family Wizard*), and divorce educational programs can be disseminated through accessible formats (e.g., Bowers et al. 2011).

In addition, online tools have been developed to assist parents in interpreting and navigating the legal system (e.g., the Parent Plan Support System [Araszkiewicz et al. 2013] and AssetDivider [Bellucci 2008]) and to ultimately come to their own decisions regarding the division of property and determination of child custody arrangements. Through the integration of artificial intelligence with game theory, separating families can be supported in negotiating and making their own decisions, thereby restoring some autonomy in what has traditionally been a disempowering process for parents (Bellucci et al. 2004). These systems can also be designed to 'learn' by using imported data to continuously self-improve service delivery and decision-making processes (e.g., Split-Up; Zeleznikow 2004). Central to the development of these tools is just and fair processes and outcomes for all involved parties, while prioritizing the present and future interests of the child (Lodder and Zeleznikow 2012). These technologies often aim to encourage cooperation between parents or to generally ease the transition from parenting together to parenting apart. The law can be complex to comprehend for a lay person, so systems that support understanding while enhancing autonomy may create spaces for empowerment and relatively easy processes toward separation.

Of particular interest, however, are FDR services as translated into online formats. In Australia, FDR is preferred to 'mediation' (Ainsworth et al. 2019) with the former defined by the *Family Law Act 1975* (Cth) as "...a process (other than a judicial process): in which a family dispute resolution practitioners helps people affected, or likely to be affected, by separation or divorce to resolve some or all of their disputes with each other; and in which the practitioner is independent of all of the parties involved in the process".[1] As such, the family dispute resolution practitioner (FDRP) reflects an independent third party who maintains a responsibility to the child and their best interests.

The change across time in Australia regarding the provision of FDR services has been gradual, commencing with the development of traditional face-to-face services at the aforementioned FRCs, to offerings of telephone dispute resolution services (TDRS; Thomson 2009), to finally the current emerging state of OFDR. The addition of each new approach increases the number of options available to families in terms of service delivery such that families have some flexibility in choosing an approach that is most suitable to their specific case requirements. In addition, as has been seen, OFDR itself is by no means monolithic—the term has been interpreted and developed as an overlying topic bringing together a range of different approaches to dispute resolution that rely on technology. For example, services can differ in terms of communication modalities (e.g., email, synchronous text-based messaging, telephone, apps, video-conferencing) and the involvement of independent third parties, such as courts or FDRPs.

The unique benefits of OFDR are many and varied, consisting not only of the advantages associated with alternative dispute resolution (ADR) but also those specific to online capabilities. Such benefits include but are not limited to: cost- and time-effectiveness; flexible options and outcomes; less adversarial; increased accessibility to quality services for rural and remote communities; solution- rather than blame-oriented; and increased access to justice (González Martín 2015; Relationships Australia 2011; Schramm and McCaulley 2012; Tait 2013).

Access to this technology and its associated benefits, however, may be hindered if the service design and implementation is not considered with due diligence for the way that culture intersects with technology. Without this consideration, these services instead become another way to exclude and oppress those who are most vulnerable. Under-researched in both Australian and international contexts are cultural considerations for online service engagement. Chapter 5 begins to address this gap in the literature by presenting the findings of a rigorous investigation into the needs of Aboriginal and Torres Strait Islander communities in Queensland, Australia. Through the development of a collaborative research partnership which adhered to participatory action research principles (Dickson and Green 2001), the research team was able to identify several best-practice recommendations for the design and implementation of a culturally and contextually responsive OFDR system. These recommendations spoke to promoting community ownership over the system, adopting community strengths-based perspectives while facilitating appropriate capacity building, acknowledging within and between cultural diversity, and taking a holistic approach to implementation. Although a time-intensive process, the creation and maintenance of genuine, ongoing partnerships with the community was identified as critical in reducing the perpetuation of colonizing practices.

[1]Family Law Act 1975 (Cth) s 10F.

The remainder of this chapter will compile and offer the lessons learned from the research presented within this book to assist in the future development and improvement of OFDR services before then identifying some of the areas in need of further investigation in order to optimize the utility of online technologies for separating families.

6.2 Lessons Learned

First and foremost, services should prioritize increasing access to justice by ensuring that online systems are working according to the child's best interest. When independent third-parties (such as FDRPs) are involved in the process, there is a greater likelihood that this principle will be respected. Careful consideration is required, however, when developing artificially intelligent software. Automated systems must be programmed to facilitate fair processes and outcomes that not only satisfy the requirement of upholding the child's wellbeing, but also take into account the parents' interests as well (Araszkiewicz et al. 2013).

Practitioners in the OFDR area must ask 'Do we have technology for which we are looking for an avenue to utilize, or do we have problems in which we should use the technology to support our decision making'. Hopefully we are now choosing the latter path. We must also address the level of automation of the OFDR. What is the role of the human in the process?

6.2.1 Considerations for Uptake

Despite increasing use of technology, FDR service providers should avoid assuming that all members of the public would be interested in engaging with online methods of service delivery if they were available. Instead, prospective clients and professionals may feel intimidation or suspicion towards technology, especially regarding systems or processes that are unfamiliar. These feelings may result from faulty assumptions and misconceptions about the technology. To understand and therefore address the content and origin of these beliefs, thorough readiness assessments should be conducted with both potential clients and staff. These assessments should take into account user competence, user knowledge (particularly for staff), attitudes toward the technology, and trust in the system. Site readiness is an equally important consideration, thereby requiring a separate readiness assessment for the technological infrastructure which assesses the system, the organizational environment in which the system will be implemented, and the readiness of the supporting organizational staff.

While respecting an individual's right to freely choose the service appropriate for their family or their practice, a number of techniques may be employed to overcome resistance to using new systems (Conley Tyler and Bretheron 2003). For example, program 'champions' within an organisation may encourage staff to experiment with the system (Markham 1998) while respected community gatekeepers may help provide endorsement among a specific client population. In addition, targeted promoting and marketing campaigns can help to increase awareness and knowledge of proposed technologies. Social media has been found as particularly useful in reaching large audiences, with the selection of the media platform tailored toward the target population (Augar and Zeleznikow 2014; Tait 2013). Finally, trust in the technology affects technology uptake and can be facilitated by the development of tools, programs, and services that are evidence-based and then the clear communication of this evidence to prospective users (Augar and Zeleznikow 2014; Bowers et al. 2011).

6.2.1.1 Client Considerations

Not all cases are suitable for intervention by and with online technologies, with more stringent inclusion criteria required by pilot studies. Careful selection and screening tools should be used to determine appropriateness for OFDR services as compared to other services (e.g., TDRS, face-to-face FDR, or court involvement). Screening tools should be evidence-based and subject to rigorous testing and staff training procedures (Relationships Australia 2011; Tait 2013). These tools should assess for case complexity and characteristics, clients' OFDR-conducive home environment, client preference and motivation, and clients' access to and competence using technology. The latter should also be confirmed via technology checks (e.g., internet connection tests) prior to allocation to the technology-enhanced service (Relationships Australia 2011).

6.2.1.2 Pre-OFDR Education

Although the current research on OFDR preparation sessions is sparse, some lessons to inform development of these systems can be drawn from existing face-to-face pre-FDR sessions as well as online separated parenting education programs, which have similar underlying principles. Online delivery of preparatory sessions should be engaging, skills-based, and should make use of the technology available. That is, multimedia should be used where appropriate, quizzes to assess understanding accompanied by feedback should be incorporated, and opportunities for shared discussion should be enabled (Bowers et al. 2011). Unlike traditional group-based pre-FDR, online approaches lack the sense of community and ability to hear and participate in shared experiences. The inclusion of group discussion boards where stories can be shared, and questions can be posed may improve upon this shortcoming to a degree (Bowers et al. 2011).

An advantage over traditional methods, however, is the potential to individualise content to specific case characteristics. For example, upon registering for the online module, clients may be required to answer a number of questions about their specific situation (e.g., presence of domestic violence, age of child, number of children, support accommodations for visual or hearing needs) which would then direct them to case-appropriate preparatory information (Bowers et al. 2011).

These sessions may also be used not only to discuss the procedural elements of FDR, but also to assist in preparation for the technical requirements of the OFDR system. As preliminary FDRP feedback suggests that clients enter their first OFDR session without having completed the requisite administrative aspects, such as changing passwords upon first log-in or completing the connection test (Relationships Australia 2011), the nature of the pre-OFDR session (i.e., the fact that it is already online) makes it an ideal setting in which to embed learning around the technical elements of OFDR participation.

6.2.1.3 Staff Considerations

When developing and implementing software, it is important not to discount the needs of the FDRP in favour of an exclusive focus on the client. OFDR will ultimately be ineffective if the preferences and requirements of the FDRPs and other staff who engage with the system are not taken into account. To this end, system development should plan for staff training, needs analysis and readiness scoping, and continued support throughout system use.

Staff training should be informed by an organizational needs analysis as well as contemporary and evidence-based research. General elements of training plans may include: transferring and adapting FDR techniques to an online platform, managing and overcoming diminished non-verbal cues, and using the software and supporting clients to use the software. Training should be intensive, experiential, and offer opportunities for ongoing learning and support across time. Practical engagement with the system is essential to successful training and preparation. Not only will staff be able to obtain a concrete understanding of the system, but it can also help to alleviate concerns or misconceptions held around the system.

FDRPs should also be trained in how to manage their on-screen presence when using video-conferencing capabilities. Due consideration should be paid to learning how to interact with the web-cam technology as well as how to adjust the physical location, lighting, and general room appearance in order to be conducive to quality OFDR sessions (Jani 2012; Relationships Australia 2011).

In addition, training should be conducted as temporally close as possible to the actual use of the system. Only minimal training may be required to achieve an appropriate level of proficiency prior to use (e.g., two full days; Relationships Australia 2011), with additional 'booster' sessions to follow where required. The answer to what level is considered 'proficient enough' should be driven by the consumer's needs. As access to quality technology becomes more widespread, the proportion of the general public who are already proficient in technology use increases, with FDRPs needing skills that match their level (Larson 2003; Relationships Australia 2011).

On-call technical support should be made available to FDRPs during the sessions and peer support networks should be developed to help consolidate and share learning, particularly in the beginning stages of system navigation (Jani 2012). Similarly, peer-led training may be appropriate once more practitioners become proficient with the system, such that less experienced FDRPs may ‘shadow’ or co-facilitate OFDR sessions with more experienced FDRPs (Lavi 2014).

To be considered appropriate to practice OFDR, FDRPs should first have robust mediation skills (Tait 2013). The learning curve associated with navigating the technology requires a solid foundation of FDR skills as not to reduce the quality of the service when compared to traditional face-to-face methods. Determining an appropriate FDR skill level may involve self-assessments, years of practice, and observational assessments to determine readiness. Additional specialized skills are required for work with culturally and linguistically diverse communities and/or working in cross-border cases. FDRPs interested in pursuing this area of work need to be aware of all-involved countries’ and/or states’ laws pertaining to mediation and family law (LaMarca 2012).

6.2.2 Considerations for Technology

Common sense dictates that due to the constantly advancing nature of technology, developers and users of online systems cannot remain complacent, instead they must continuously respond and adapt to changes in information technology research and practice. Systems need to engage in ongoing monitoring, evaluation, and improvement processes either through in-built self-improvement processes (e.g., as in Split-Up; Zeleznikow 2004) or through periodic and systematic developer intervention. On the latter, development of this technology should not occur in isolation but rather should be the result of a multidisciplinary effort representing a range of different interests, knowledges, and perspectives, including representatives from artificial intelligence, law, computer technology, and family relationship domains. The technology vendor responsible for the online solution, should be selected with care and open, continuous communication should be established early in the relationship (Relationships Australia 2011).

Systems should also be co-designed with the intended clients of the platforms, with subsequent iterative cycles of planning, testing, feedback, and adjustment (Knight and Hunter 2013; Relationships Australia 2011). Such processes would help to develop programs that are responsive and relevant to the needs of their clients.

The adjustment of an existing online system or the development of new capabilities should also always be subject to extensive trialing and testing periods prior to implementation. Time and resources should be allocated for this process during the planning stages of project development. Central to the development and evaluation should be the consideration of the user. That is, the system should be easy and comfortable to use, trust with the technology should be forthcoming, and at no point should the technology, this 'fourth party' (Katsh and Rifkin 2001), detract from the overall objective (that is, a fair and just outcome for disputing parties). Less important but also to be under consideration are the aesthetics of the user interface. The deliverance of these objectives can be facilitated through user feedback, as previously described.

Regarding system use, users should avoid assuming the infallibility of the technology after it has been subjected to rigorous testing. Even the most extensive of testing procedures cannot resolve all issues prior to implementation of the system. As such, FDRPs should discuss and develop back-up plans with their clients during pre-session inductions or intakes in the event of technology malfunctioning (Tait 2013). During the planning phases, the team developing the technology may also wish to adhere to principles of 'granular redundancy'. As described in the RAQ OFDR pilot program, this principle allows for connection to be maintained via audio-only means when video-conferencing capabilities are disrupted.

OFDR platforms in particular should be developed to allow for the use of multiple technologies as a means to not only accommodate different clients' needs but also to reflect various stages of the FDR process (Tait 2013). For example, email may be used for administrative activities while video-conferencing software may be used for the actual mediation session. The unique tools and features afforded by technology should also be optimized in order to make the most of the unique, value-added capabilities (Lavi 2014). At all times, the technology and all its associated components should be under the control of the FDRP to minimize misuse.

6.2.2.1 Ethics and Safety

In addition to the usual ethical considerations involved in facilitating FDR processes, there are further concerns that should be addressed and managed when using technology to assist in family disputes. Of utmost concern is privacy and confidentiality of information. The choice in technology used in the service needs to balance the security capabilities of technology against user familiarity of technology. That is, one may need to sacrifice easy accessible and cheaper technical solutions for more secure options (Jani 2012). A risk-averse approach should therefore be applied when creating online solutions for family dispute purposes.

Multi-layered and secure processes should be incorporated into the technology through dual authentication procedures such that the FDRP can verify the identity of the client(s) and the client(s) can verify the credentials of the FDRP (Augar and Zeleznikow 2014; Conley Tyler and Bretheron 2003; Relationships Australia 2011). The latter may be facilitated via professional websites to which the client can be directed to view and assess the relevant qualifications of the third-party (e.g., Augar and Zeleznikow 2014).

The steps taken to protect confidentiality and the limits of these provisions should be clearly communicated, in plain language, to the users of the technology. Potential clients should be able to review these stipulations prior to service engagement in order to make informed decisions about whether this service is appropriate for their needs. Service costs should be made explicit at this time, particularly those additional costs involved in the use of online systems (e.g., data downloads). In online mediation processes, these conditions may be communicated within an 'Agreement to Mediate' form which is sighted and signed by all parties prior to participation in FDR (Jani 2012). The document should be tailored to online service delivery and may also include expectations for online behavior, or 'netiquette'. This form and the considerations for confidentiality should be explained at length in private, individual sessions with each party.

Online technologies have the potential to be netocratic (that is, providing equality among parties in the online environment), however a FDRP must remain vigilant for power imbalances (Barsky 2016). Parties may have unequal skills in using technology, they may have access to different quality technology, or one party may have used technology as a tool for violence against the other; all of these can, and should, be picked up at the screening stage. Regardless, risk management requires constant assessment throughout the OFDR process and FDRPs should be transparent if they believe that suitability for online technologies has changed.

Ethical considerations of the technology should also take into account the safety and security of the FDRP or other third-party involvement. Care should be taken to avoid revealing the third party's last name or their private email addresses, and boundaries should also be clearly set and adhered to regarding expectations for service delivery. For example, in services that offer asynchronous modes of communication, the FDRP should manage expectations around when responses are to be received.

6.3 Recommendations for Future Research and Practice

Following the extensive research undertaken to outline the current state of OFDR research and practice for this book, a number of recommendations can be proposed to assist in the continued advancement of this field.

6.3.1 Mobile Device-Supported OFDR

Attention and resources should be invested in investigating the efficacy and effectiveness of using mobile devices for OFDR and related services. As more of the general public in Australia and worldwide obtain access to powerful hand-held technology, researchers and service providers should capitalize on this opportunity to understand how FDR services can be adapted to meet this gap in the market. Already identified in this book are current co-parenting and communication-enhancing apps designed to address the needs of separated families, however the application of FDR services or negotiation support systems on mobile devices has yet to be explored. Mobile applications are likely to offer additional tools to enhance the wellbeing and decision-making of transitioning families that both complement and are distinct from current approaches (e.g., web-based, telephone, and face-to-face). However, Schmitz and Wing (2020) caution that while the option of mobile-supported OFDR can increase access to justice, it may also have the unintended effect of reducing privacy and safety. The advantages and disadvantages of this technology therefore warrants further review.

6.3.2 The Suitability of Domestic Violence Cases to OFDR

There is currently mixed opinion in the research as to whether cases of domestic violence are appropriate for OFDR intervention. Although comprehensive screening tools and case-by-case assessments will always be necessary to determine suitability to OFDR, there is a need for systematic research to identify the conditions under which the presence of domestic violence may or may not disrupt achievement of FDR objectives. For example, does OFDR effectiveness depend on the severity of the violence, the type of violence inflicted, the current geographical proximity of the parties, and whether the violence is ongoing or how recently violence ceased (Tait 2013)?

In addition, the roles and responsibilities of the mediator when domestic violence is disclosed or suspected must be carefully considered. Extending on discussions in Chap. 3 regarding power imbalances, one must also consider the power of the mediator in directing and controlling the narrative of the FDR session(s) (Flynn 2005; Grillo 1991; Hughes 1995; Ver Steegh 2003). The very act of managing power imbalances between the disputing parties is argued to disrupt the idea of the mediator as a passive and neutral party (Grillo 1991). The offline FDR literature contemplates which of the disputing parties the mediator meets with first, that is, whose version of events do they hear first, and what implications this decision has for ongoing mediation processes within domestic violence cases (Flynn 2005; Rossi et al. 2017). How is this consideration extrapolated to the online environment?

Offline FDR literature also presents insights regarding post-mediation contact. The mediator must be mindful that the interaction between the disputing parties may continue after the session has concluded. In domestic violence situations, there are serious concerns raised about the potential for physical violence to ensue following mediation (Field 1998; Grillo 1991; Rossi et al. 2017). These concerns may be mitigated in OFDR if there is geographical distance between parties, however there are other types of violence and controlling behaviour that may occur.

Despite a significant minority of registering clients in the RAQ study reporting the presence of past or current domestic violence in the relationship for which they were seeking mediation, minimal attention has been dedicated to understanding how violence impacts OFDR engagement. For instance, surveys with 152 domestic violence advocates and 46 victims show that technology—including phones, tablets, computers, and social networking websites—is commonly used in intimate partner stalking (Woodlock 2016). Here, technology was used to create a sense of the perpetrator's omnipresence, and to isolate, punish, and humiliate domestic violence victims. Perpetrators also threatened to share sexualized content online to humiliate victims. The prevalence of technology facilitated domestic abuse can therefore prove a major drawback to engaging in FDR.

Alternatively, Rimelspach (2001) argues that there does not seem to be a clear case to reject mediation for family disputes, despite the prevalence of domestic violence. He claims that one of the key factors in the area of dispute resolution is to offer as many alternatives to parties as possible, so that the most appropriate method can be chosen for each case. Further, Rimelspach stresses that considering the numerous benefits that mediation can offer over the adversarial system, it would seem a senseless loss to exclude all court mediation programs as an option for individuals whose interpersonal relationships contain elements of domestic violence.

Future research may also consider whether separate guidelines need to be developed for online practice in cases of domestic violence as well as including specialized components in staff training (Ainsworth et al. 2019).

6.3.3 Expanding the Capabilities of OFDR

Many of the OFDR systems cited in this book have been pilot projects and have therefore been subjected to strict restrictions in order to maximise service quality. As such, there is a need to explore the full capacities and identify the limitations of OFDR systems. For example, although it has been posited that hybrid models may be effective (e.g., González Martín 2015), there is no evidence to-date that combinations of face-to-face and online modalities within the same case are beneficial for clients. The few studies that have included both approaches have compared them against each other (e.g., Rossi et al. 2017; Schramm and McCaulley 2012) as opposed to including a condition in which both were combined.

In addition, there remains a gap in understanding whether OFDR systems are capable of managing more than three parties (i.e., the FDRP and the two disputing parents) and what adjustments may need to be made to the system to ensure that the technology remains seamless, cost-effective, and of a high quality when additional parties are involved. As one example, several OFDR systems mention making accommodations for interpreters and other support persons to be present during the mediation session, however it remains to be seen how the logistics of this arrangement are navigated.

Similarly, the voices of the children in question could be considered, with implications for their involvement in online environments. Research would need to determine the advantages and disadvantages of their inclusion in the service, the considerations and concerns for engagement in online as opposed to face-to-face FDR, best practices and guidelines for children's inclusion, and at what age a child may be considered suitable to have input into the process.

6.3.4 Cultural and Contextual Considerations

Although there has been much anecdotal evidence about the application of technology to disempowered groups to increase access to justice, there has been minimal investigation into what this looks like when applied. Following best practices outlined in Chap. 5, research with vulnerable and disadvantaged groups should seek collaboration and participatory approaches to ensure appropriateness in development, implementation, and evaluation. These practices should encourage community ownership and support self-determination to guide decision-making concerning the system. Guiding these processes should be the commitment to developing technology that provides spaces in which empowerment can occur, rather than exacerbating oppression and inequality (e.g., the 'digital divide' [Cullen 2001] prevalent in Aboriginal and Torres Strait Islander communities).

Rao (2004) outlines some considerations for system design and mediator preparedness that should be examined further using evidence-based methods. For instance, she discusses the capabilities of ODR services to accommodate language options other than English, how limiting non-verbal cues can impact meaning-making, and the cultural competencies of the mediator to be able to interpret cultural nuances. She also brings awareness to the fact that the online environment is itself a unique cultural setting that must also be appreciated and understood.

While Rainey (2012) echoes some of these points, he cautions not to potentially overstate the effects of cultural differences on ODR engagement (i.e., a "Type II" error. He distinguishes a "Type I" error as the ignorance of cultural differences.). Further, while acknowledging the need for mediators to make gains towards "cultural competency", he also issues a reminder that mediators themselves bring their own cultural biases and beliefs to the session. Of note is the culturally embedded professional training of the mediator which has been argued to predominantly take place within the 'North American Model of mediation' and subsequently has implications for the generalisability of these practices.

6.3.5 Advancing Research and Evaluation

As a final recommendation which bears relevance on all previous points is that more methodologically rigorous research and evaluation is required to provide evidence for the effectiveness of OFDR. It will be difficult to encourage widespread adoption of technologically-enhanced dispute resolution services if the evidence on which the argument for use is founded is fallible and/or sparse. Additionally, in order to make accurate decisions regarding case suitability for OFDR and other online services for families, more research needs to be conducted with a range of client populations, including same-sex couples, culturally and linguistically diverse groups, and individuals who have hearing and visual impairments or other support requirements.

This research should include a longitudinal focus such that outcomes can be assessed across time.

OFDR systems of the future should provide the following facilities:

1. Case management: the system should allow users to enter information, ask them for appropriate data and provide for templates to initiate the dispute;
2. Triaging: the system should make decisions on how important it is to act in a timely manner and where to send the dispute;
3. Advisory tools: the system should provide tools for reality testing: these could include, books, articles, reports of cases, copies of legislation and videos; there would also be calculators (such as to advise upon child support) and BATNA advisory; systems (to inform disputants of the likely outcome if the dispute were to be decided by decision-maker e.g. judge, arbitrator or ombudsman);
4. Communication tools—for negotiation, mediation, conciliation or facilitation. This could involve shuttle mediation if required;
5. Decision Support Tools—if the disputants cannot resolve their conflict, software using game theory or artificial intelligence can be used to facilitate trade-offs;
6. Drafting software: if and once a negotiation is reached, software can be used to draft suitable agreements;

Of course no single dispute is likely to require all six processes. However, the development of such a hybrid ODR system would be very significant.

6.4 Conclusion

Although as compared to the history of alternative dispute resolution in Australia OFDR is relatively young, the latter has piqued public interest and engagement which suggests the fulfilment of a community need. From modest beginnings in online-originating consumer disputes (Ebner and Zeleznikow 2016), the vision for online capabilities has expanded over time to include flexible options for a range of conflicts and concerns. The capacities and function of future tools and services are yet to be known, but likely only to further multiply the options available to the consumer. As Conley Tyler and Bretheron (2003) note: "The search for more convenient, cost-effective, efficient and durable ways of resolving disputes will continue for as long as disputes exist" (p. 3).

Indeed, a previously unknown and unexpected force has recently driven technological advancements in mediation service delivery. During the writing of this book COVID-19 was declared a pandemic across the globe. Although the long-term impacts of this public health issue remain to be seen, Sourdin and Zeleznikow (2020) have discussed the early trends affecting the courts and ODR. Social distancing guidelines have prevented in-person dispute resolution which has forced the uptake of technology to continue delivering services. Technological innovation has increased in response, however the authors question the readiness of the justice system in integrating these technologies into their service delivery approaches.

Integration of ODR into the courts was already growing, however these events have expedited demand. Prior to COVID-19, leaders in eCourt innovation included Canada's *Civil Resolution Tribunal*, the United Kingdom's *Her Majesty's Online Courts*, China's *Hangzhou Internet* Court, and the United States' use of *Matterhorn* for small claims, family disputes, and traffic citations. Both Schmitz (2019) and Sela (2019) have identified a number of considerations that should be taken into account in eCourt system design in order to make it efficient, fair, accessible, and user-friendly.

Giglione (2019) argues that there have been three stages of ODR expansion since its conception in the 1990s, and that a fourth stage is currently underway. This stage is defined by a continued growth in ODR usage across the world, the development of standards and regulations, and an integration of AI with dispute resolution. Pearlstein (2012) has also noted an increasing trend of individual practitioners, separate from organisations, providing OFDR services. Additional trends that may see future growth include crowd-sourced ODR (which are argued to be, in their current state, more like focus groups than ODR but have the potential for development) and hybrid systems combining offline and online dispute resolution processes (Sela 2017).

While it is claimed the online services will not and should not ever replace traditional face-to-face mediation and rather technology-enhanced tools should be another option in a mediator's toolbox (e.g., Augar and Zeleznikow 2014; González Martín 2015; Jani 2012; Knight and Hunter 2013), the rise of technology in alternative dispute resolution appears inevitable (Larson 2003). To this end, it is even more crucial that high quality research be conducted in order to inform the development of technologies that enhance mediation outcomes and the wellbeing of separating families.

It has been the intention of this book to outline the current state of OFDR services as they are used within Australia. Although Australia has been identified as a leader in ODR and OFDR services, a comprehensive documentation of its history in the field, its services, and its unique considerations for service development and provision. This book has brought together a collection of evidence, both theoretical knowledge and case examples, to elucidate the how OFDR is flourishing both in Australia and worldwide in order to meet the needs of a technologically advancing and dispersed population. With an understanding of the foundations on which OFDR was formed, program developers can ensure that they are creating and implementing services that are continuously improving. Further, through a rigorous synthesis of current research and practices, this book has been able to present guidelines for future service development that enhances fair and just outcomes and the efficiency with which those outcomes are obtained. Through this research process, this book has highlighted gaps requiring amendment to show the worth of OFDR to both public and private potential consumers and to maximise the effectiveness of these services. It is inevitable that the OFDR landscape in Australia and abroad will change dramatically in the coming years, however the learnings, recommendations, and guide points in this book will continue to offer important insights to professionals who are looking to enter this rewarding and exciting field.

References

Ainsworth N, Zeleznikow L, Zeleznikow J (2019) Readiness for online family dispute resolution. Int J Online Disp Resol 6:243–263

Araszkiewicz M, Łopatkiewicz A, Zienkiewicz A (2013) Parent Plan Support System – context, functions and knowledge base. Paper presented at The International Conference on Business Information Systems Heidelberg, Berlin, Springer, 19-20 June 2013

Augar N, Zeleznikow J (2014) Developing online support and counseling to enhance family dispute resolution in Australia. Group Decis Negot 23:515–532

Barsky AE (2016) The ethics of app-assisted family mediation. Conflict Resol Q 34:31–42

Bellucci E (2008) AssetDivider: a new mediation tool in Australian family law. In: Proceedings of the First International Working Conference on Human Factors and Computational Models in Negotiation, Delft University of Technology, Delft, 8-9 December 2008

Bellucci E, Lodder AR, Zeleznikow J (2004) Integrating artificial intelligence, argumentation and game theory to develop an online dispute resolution environment. Paper presented at the 16th IEEE International Conference on Tools with Artificial Intelligence, Boca Raton, Florida, 15-17 November

Bowers JR, Mitchell ET, Hardesty JL, Hughes R Jr (2011) A review of online divorce education programs. Family Court Rev 49:776–787

Conley Tyler M, Bretheron D (2003) Developing an online mediation culture: The fourth generation of online ADR. Paper presented at the 2nd Asia-Pacific Mediation Forum, Singapore, 19-22 November

Cullen R (2001) Addressing the digital divide. Online Info Rev 25:311–320

Dickson G, Green K (2001) The external researcher in participatory action research. Educ Action Res 9:243–260

Ebner N, Zeleznikow J (2016) No sheriff in town: governance for the ODR field. Negot J 32:297–323

Field R (1998) Mediation and the art of power (im)balancing. QUT Law J 12:264–273

Flynn D (2005) The social worker as family mediator: Balancing power in cases involving family violence. Aust Soc Work 58:407–418

Giglione T (2019) Recent growth and developments on online dispute resolution in Southeast Asia. World Mediation Organisation Conflict Insight. https://worldmediation.org/recent-growth-and-developments-on-online-dispute-resolution-in-southeast-asia/

González Martín N (2015) International parental child abduction and mediation. Anuario Mexicano de Derecho Internacional 15:353–412

Grillo T (1991) The mediation alternative: process dangers for women. Yale Law J 100:1545–1610

Hughes SH (1995) Elizabeth's story: exploring power imbalances in divorce mediation. Georgetown J Leg Ethics 8:553–596

Jani S (2012) Mediating from a distance: suggested practice guidelines for family mediators, 2nd edn. MediateBC, Vancouver

Katsh E, Rifkin J (2001) Introducing the fourth party: the critical role of technology. In: Online dispute resolution: resolving conflicts in cyberspace. Jossey-Bass, San Francisco, pp 93–116

Knight K, Hunter C (2013) Using technology in service delivery to families, children and young people, no. 17. Child Family Community Australia (CFCA). https://aifs.gov.au/cfca/publications/using-technology-service-delivery-families-children

LaMarca J (2012) Virtually possible - using the internet to facilitate custody and parenting beyond relocation. Rutgers Comput Technol Law J 38:146–172

Larson DA (2003) Online dispute resolution: do you know where your children are? Negot J 19:199–205

Lavi D (2014) No more click-click in here: e-mediation in divorce disputes-the reality and the desirable. Cardozo J Conflict Resol 16:479–541

Lodder AR, Zeleznikow J (2012) Artificial intelligence and online dispute resolution. In: Wahab M, Katsh E, Rainey D (eds) Online dispute resolution: theory and practice. Eleven International Publishers, Ten Haag, Netherlands, pp 61–82

Markham SK (1998) A longitudinal examination of how champions influence others to support their projects. J Prod Innov Manage 15:490–504

Nicholson A, Harrison M (2000) Family law and the family court of Australia: experiences of the first 25 years. Melbourne Univ Law Rev 24:757–783

Parkinson P (2013) The idea of family relationship centres in Australia. Family Court Rev 51:195–213

Pearlstein A, Hanson B, Ebner N (2012) ODR in North America. In: Abdel Wahab MS, Katsh E, Rainey D (eds) Online dispute resolution: theory and practice. Eleven International Publishing, The Hague, pp 431–452

Rainey D (2012) ODR and culture. In: Abdel Wahab MS, Katsh E, Rainey D (eds) Online dispute resolution: theory and practice. Eleven International Publishing, The Hague, pp 185–201

Rao S (2004) The cultural vacuum in online dispute resolution. Paper presented at the Third Annual Forum on Online Dispute Resolution

Relationships Australia (2011) Development and evaluation of online family dispute resolution capabilities. https://www.ag.gov.au/Publications/Pages/OnlineFamilyDisputeResolutionEvaluation.aspx

Rimelspach RL (2001) Mediating family disputes in a world with domestic violence: how to devise a safe and effective court-connected mediation program. Ohio State J Disp Resol 17:95–112

Rossi FS, Holtzworth-Munroe A, Applegate AG, Beck CJ, Adams JM, Hale DF (2017) Shuttle and online mediation: a review of available re-search and implications for separating couples reporting intimate partner violence or abuse. Family Court Rev 55:390–403

Schmitz AJ (2019) Expanding access to remedies through E-court initiatives. Buffalo Law Rev 67:89–163

Schmitz AJ, Wing L (2020) Beneficial and ethical ODR for family issues. Fam Court Rev. Forthcoming

Schramm DG, McCaulley G (2012) Divorce education for parents: a comparison of online and in-person delivery methods. J Divorce Remarriage 53:602–617

Sela A (2017) The effect of online technologies on dispute resolution system design: antecedents, current trends, and future directions. Lewis Clark Law Rev 21:635–683

Sela A (2019) e-Nudging justice: the role of digital choice architecture in online courts. J Disp Resol 2:128–163

Sourdin T, Zeleznikow J (2020) Courts, mediation and COVID-19. Aust Bus Law Rev 48(2):138–158

Tait C (2013) Evaluation of the Distance Family Mediation Project: report on Phase III of the technology-assisted family mediation project, MediateBC, Canada. http://www.mediatebc.com/about-mediation/mediating-at-a-distance.aspx

Thomson M (2009) Annual report of the telephone dispute resolution service to the attorney general. Relationships Australia, Queensland

Ver Steegh N (2003) Yes, no, and maybe: informed decision making about divorce mediation in the presence of domestic violence. William Mary J Woman Law 9:145–206

Woodlock D (2016) The abuse of technology in domestic violence and stalking. Violence Against Women 23:584–602

Zeleznikow J (2004) The split-up project: induction, context and knowledge discovery in law. Law. Probab Risk 3:147–168

Glossary

Adjusted Winner Adjusted Winner is a two party point allocation procedure that distributes items or issues to people on the premise of whoever values the item or issue more. The two disputants are required to explicitly indicate how much they value each of the different issues by distributing 100 points across the range of issues in dispute. In this paradigm, it is assumed there are k discrete issues in dispute, each of which is assumed divisible. The Adjusted Winner paradigm is a fair and equitable procedure because at the end of allocation, each party will have accrued the same number of points

Arbitration Arbitration is an adversarial process whereby an independent third party (or parties), after hearing submissions from the disputants makes an award binding upon the parties

Artificial Intelligence Artificial Intelligence involves the study of automated human intelligence. This includes both practically-oriented research, such as building computer applications that perform tasks requiring human intelligence, and fundamental research, such as determining how to represent knowledge in a computer-comprehensible form

AssetDivider AssetDivider is a system developed to meet the needs of family dispute resolution practitioners at Relationships Australia (Queensland). It generalises Family_Winner by including financial values of property and allowing mediators to bias the negotiation (so as to meet the *paramount interests of the children)* in favour of one party to the negotiation

Asynchronous Communication In asynchronous communication, parties do not take part in the discussion at the same time

***BATNA*—Know Your Best Alternative to a Negotiated Agreement** The reason you negotiate with someone is to produce better results than would otherwise occur. If you are unaware of what results you could obtain if the negotiations are unsuccessful, you run the risk of entering into an agreement that you would be better off rejecting; or rejecting an agreement you would be better off entering into

E. Wilson-Evered, J. Zeleznikow, *Online Family Dispute Resolution*, Law, Governance and Technology Series 45,
https://doi.org/10.1007/978-3-030-64645-5

Best Interests of the Child Section 60CA of the *Family Law Act 1975* (Cth) states that, "in deciding whether to make a particular parenting order in relation to a child, a court must regard the best interests of the child as the paramount consideration"

Brainstorming In brainstorming, the parties, with or without the mediator's participation, generate many possible solution before deciding which of those best fulfill the parties' joint interests

Burden of Proof In the law of evidence, the burden of proof is the necessity or duty of affirmatively proving a fact or facts in dispute on an issue raised between the parties in a cause. Except as otherwise provided by the law, the burden of proof requires proof by a preponderance of the evidence. In a criminal case, the government, beyond a reasonable doubt, must prove all the elements of the crime. Except in cases of tax fraud, the burden of proof is on the balance of probabilities. In a tax case, the burden of proof in a tax case is generally on the taxpayer

Common Law Common law is the legal tradition that evolved in England from the eleventh century onwards. Its principles appear for the most part in reported judgments, usually of the higher courts, in relation to specific fact situations arising in disputes that courts have adjudicated. Common law systems are open, in the sense that new rules may be created or imported for new facts

Conciliation Conciliation as compared to mediation is a process by which the participants, together with the assistance of a support person, systematically isolate disputed issues in order to develop options, consider alternatives, and reach a consensual settlement that will accommodate their needs. The conciliator generally provides advice to help resolve the dispute

Confirming Evidence Trap The notion that disputants strongly adhere to positions taken and are more likely to actively collect information that confirms the validity of their position, and downplay or ignore information that refutes their choice

Data Mining Pattern A data mining pattern is interesting if: (a) the pattern is easily understood by humans; (b) the pattern is valid (with some degree of certainty) on new or test data; (c) the pattern is potentially useful; the pattern is novel

Data Mining Data mining is a problem-solving methodology that finds a logical or mathematical description, eventually of a complex nature, of patterns and regularities in a set of data

Decision Analysis Decision analysis generated from statistical decision theory, is a methodology typically used to support decision makers actively in assessing alternative courses of action

Decision Tree A decision tree is an explicit representation of all scenarios that can result from a given decision. The root of the tree represents the initial situation, whilst each path from the root corresponds to one possible scenario

DEUS DEUS is a template-based system that displays the level of disagreement, with respect to each item, between disputants. The model underpinning the program calculates the level of agreement and disagreement between the litigants' goals at any given time. The disputants reach a negotiated settlement when the difference between the goals is reduced to nil. DEUS is useful for gaining an understanding of what issues are in dispute and the extent of the dispute over these issues

Digital Divide The digital divide is the gulf between those who have ready access to computers and the Internet, and those who do not

Discretion Discretion is a power or right conferred upon decision-makers to act according to the dictates of their own judgement and conscience, uncontrolled by the judgement or conscience of others

Divorce Education Programs The overarching goal of divorce education is to help parents and children cope with divorce, Programs are administered in one of three ways: by contractors from public or private agencies, institutions of higher education, or mental health practitioners; by a collaboration of court workers and contractors; or by court workers. Three types of attendance policies exist: state or locally mandated, judge determined, or voluntary. Voluntary and mandatory programs deliver similar content, with mandatory programs focusing more on the effects of parents' conflictual interactions on children

Expanding the Pie Expanding or enlarging the pie involves the parties in a dispute creating additional resources so that both sides can maintain their major goals

Expert System Expert systems are computer programs capable of providing advice and functioning at the standard of (and sometimes even at a higher standard than) human experts in given fields

Family Dispute Resolution Practitioner An Australian family dispute resolution practitioner is an independent person who helps people affected by separation to resolve their parenting disputes. A FDR practitioner you must meet the accreditation standards in the Family Law (Family Dispute Resolution Practitioners) Regulations 2008

Family Law Act (1975) The Act, which came into effect in January 1976, introduced no-fault divorce and espoused a holistic approach to dispute resolution, with the setting up of a specialist family court complete with court-attached conciliation and counselling The best known feature of the Act was the introduction of no-fault divorce. The Act recognised that both parents have rights and responsibilities over their children after separation, unless a court orders otherwise. This requirement for both parents to care for their children led to the need for parents to continue having a relationship following their divorce. Therefore, alternate forms of dispute resolution needed to be developed

Family Relationship Centres As a major step in the Family Law Reforms of 2006, the Australian government provided financial support to open a series of 65 family relationship centres. The centres were funded to provide information, advice, and dispute resolution to help people reach agreement on parenting arrangements without the need to go court

Family Winner Family_Winner asks disputants to list the items in dispute and to attach importance values to indicate how significant it is that the disputants be awarded each of the items. The system uses this information to form trade-off rules. The trade-off rules are then used to allocate issues according to a "logrolling" strategy

Fifth Party In an ODR environment, the fifth party represents the provider of the technology

Fourth Party In an ODR environment, the fourth party is the Information Technology that supports the dispute resolution

Game Theory Game theory is a branch of applied mathematics that provides advice about the optimal distribution of resources. In the case of a negotiation, the goal of game theory is to develop the best outcome related to the choices each person has made

Governance Governance involves applying policies, proper implementation, and continuous monitoring of an organisation

Hybrid Reasoning A hybrid reasoning system combines facets of one or more of the following representation schemes into a single integrated programming environment: logical, procedural, network and structured. It usually includes object orientation, rules for representing heuristic knowledge and support for a variety of search strategies

Inductive Reasoning Inductive reasoning is the process of moving from specific cases to general rules. A rule induction system is given examples of a problem where the outcome is known. When it has been given several examples, the rule induction system can create rules that are true from the example cases. The rules can then be used to assess other cases where the outcome is not known

Inference Inference is the process of deriving conclusions from premises

Influence Diagram An influence diagram gives a simple visual representation of a decision problem. It provides a technique for identifying and displaying the essential elements of a decision: namely the values of issues and how they influence each other. It uses nodes to represent uncertain quantities or random variables. Lines joining the nodes represent conditional dependence/independence between the nodes

Information System An information system is a computer system whose basic purpose is to represent/store or manipulate data, information or knowledge

Integrative Negotiation In integrative approaches to negotiation, problems are seen as having more potential solutions than are immediately obvious and the goal is to *expand the pie* before dividing it. Parties attempt to accommodate as many interests of each of the parties as possible, leading to the so-called *win-win* or *all gain* approach

Interest Based Negotiation In an interest-based orientation, the disputants attempt to reconcile their underlying interests

Issue An issue is a legal factor that was known to be relevant to the outcome of a case

Justice Based Negotiation A right or justice-based orientation relies upon a determination of who is right in accordance with some accepted guidelines for behaviour

Learning Learning is any change in a system that allows it to perform better the second time on repetition of the same task drawn from the same population

Litigation Litigation is a contest in a court of law for the purpose of enforcing a right or seeking a remedy

Logrolling Logrolling is a process in which participants look collectively at multiple issues to find issues that one party considers more important than does the opposing party. Logrolling is successful if the parties concede issues to which they give low importance values

Machine Learning Machine learning is that subsection of learning in which the artificial intelligence system attempts to learn automatically

Mediation Mediation is a process by which the participants, together with the assistance of a neutral person or persons, systematically isolate disputed issues in order to develop options, consider alternatives, and reach a consensual settlement that will accommodate their needs

Negotiation Negotiation is a process where the parties involved modify their demands to achieve a mutually acceptable compromise. The essence of negotiation is that there is no third party whose role is to act as facilitator or umpire in

Netiquitte Netiquette is the use of good manners in online communication

Netocracy The Netocracy is a perceived global upper-class that bases its power on a technological advantage and networking skills

Online Family Dispute Resolution Online Family Dispute Resolution is the provision of Family Dispute Resolution services over the internet

Optimistic Overconfidence People have a tendency to develop an overly optimistic view on their chances in disputes. This process is referred to as 'optimistic overconfidence', because disputants have unrealistic optimistic expectations about the validity of their judgements

Our Family Wizard The OurFamilyWizard website and mobile applications provide a neutral space for separated parents to schedule and track parenting time, share information, and create a record of communication

Paramount Interests of the Child Section 60CA of the Australian *Family Law Act 1975* (Cth) states that, "in deciding whether to make a particular parenting order in relation to a child, a court must regard the best interests of the child as the paramount consideration."

Parenting Plans A parenting plan is an informal agreement that the parents make in order to determine how they will continue to care for and support their children when they are no longer together

Pareto Optimal Given a set of alternative allocations for a set of agents, a movement from one allocation to another that can make at least one agent better off without making any other agent worse off is called a Pareto improvement. An allocation is Pareto optimal when no further Pareto improvements can be made

Power Based Negotiation A power-based orientation often takes the form of a power contest where each side strives to force the other to concede

Power Imbalances A power imbalance in negotiation occurs whenever there is a significant imbalance in negotiation power between the parties

Pre FDR Education Pre-FDR education is an information session informing FDR clients about the FDR process and encouraging them to focus upon the needs of their children

Principled Negotiation Principled negotiation promotes deciding issues on their merits rather than through a haggling process focussed on what each side says it will and will not do

Pro Se Litigant A pro se litigant is one who represents her/himself

Proof Beyond Reasonable Doubt Proof beyond a reasonable doubt is such proof as precludes every reasonable hypothesis except that which it tends to support and which is wholly consistent with the defendant's guilt and inconsistent with any other rational conclusion

Proof by a Fair Preponderance Of The Evidence Proof by a fair preponderance of the evidence is the standard of proof required in civil cases; a decision is made according to that evidence which as a whole is more credible and convincing to the mind and which best accords with reason and probability

Reactive Devaluation Reactive devaluation in a negotiation refers to the fact that the very offer of a particular proposal or concession—especially if the offer comes from an adversary—may diminish its apparent value or attractiveness in the eyes of the recipient

Readiness for Family Dispute Resolution Zartman argues that parties resolve their conflict only when they are ready to do so—when alternative, usually unilateral, means of achieving a satisfactory result are blocked and the parties find themselves in an uncomfortable and costly predicament. At that point, they grab on to proposals that usually have been in the air for a long time and that only now appear attractive. In FDR: a. It is unwise to conduct the FDR immediately after partners separate as it can be useful for the parties to receive some counselling; b. It is useful to have the parties separate financial and children's issues and to sort out their finances before FDR commences; c. The FDR process tends to be more successful once the initial anger has dissipated; d. Most importantly mediations tend to be more successful once power imbalances have been addressed. This process may involve shuttle mediation and should only occur if no safety issues are present

Satisficing Satisficing is a decision-making strategy of selecting the first alternative discovered that happens to be sufficient with respect to some minimal criteria

Shuttle Mediation Shuttle mediation is the process of mediators assisting the parties involved in a conflict to reach agreement without them being present in the same room at a mediation meeting

Skype Skype is public domain software that enables individuals and businesses to make free video and voice calls, send instant messages and share files with other Skype users

Smartsettle SmartSettle is an interactive computer program developed to assist those involved in negotiating agreements among parties having conflicting objectives. It can be used during the negotiation process by opposing parties or by a professional mediator. On the basis of information provided to the program, in confidence, by each party, it can help all parties identify feasible alternatives, if any exist, that should be preferred to each party's proposal. If such alternatives do not exist, the program can help parties develop counter proposals

Split-Up SPLIT-UP is a hybrid rule based/ neural network system that uses textbooks, heuristics, expert advice and cases to model that part of the Family Law Act 1975 (Australia) which deals with property division. Explanation is provided through the use of Toulmin argument structures.

Statistical Reasoning In contrast to symbolic reasoning, statistical reasoning derives its results by checking whether or not there is a statistical correlation between two events. Examples of statistical reasoning include neural networks and rule induction systems. Whilst rule based systems are considered to be examples of symbolic reasoning; the rules are often derived using statistical tests

Synchronous Communication Synchronous communication is direct communication, with a minimal time interval between the moment one party makes a comment in a discussion, and the other party receives this message

Telephone Dispute Resolution The Australian Telephone Dispute Resolution Service (TDRS) commenced in 2007. Potential clients cannot directly contact or self-refer to the TDRS; rather they need to be referred either through the Family Relationship Advice Line, a Family Relationships Centre, or any other government-funded Family Dispute Resolution provider. On referral from FRAL or a FRC, clients discuss their requirements with TDRS staff and if appropriate register their dispute

Trust-Convenience-Expertise Triangle The Trust-Convenience-Expertise Triangle reflects the elements that should be present in any ODR system. The parties using the system should trust it, the use of the system has to be convenient, and the system should offer expertise

Utility Function A utility function is a subjective measurement that expresses the relative value of different package by using a numerical scale

Video Conferencing Video conferencing in ODR allows synchronous face-to-face communication between disputants and the neutral. Images are two-dimensional, and, as eye contact is via a fixed camera, some information gained from eye contact is lost. Lagging can create delays in responses and lead to a perception of hesitancy. Physical movement may be constrained by camera angles and bandwidth constraints. Video conferencing also fails to convey other sensory data such as touch and smell

Zero Sum Game A zero-sum game describes a situation in which a participant's gain or loss is exactly balanced by the losses or gains of the other participant(s)

Zone of Possible Agreement The zone of possible agreement (ZOPA), in a negotiation, indicates the joint area or range where an agreement can be met to which both parties can agree. Within this zone, an agreement is possible. Outside of the zone, no amount of negotiation will yield an agreement

Index

E. Wilson-Evered, J. Zeleznikow, *Online Family Dispute Resolution*, Law, Governance and Technology Series 45,
https://doi.org/10.1007/978-3-030-64645-5

The manufacturer's authorised representative in the EU is Springer Nature Customer Service Centre GmbH, Europaplatz 3, 69115 Heidelberg, Germany. If you have any concerns regarding our products, please contact ProductSafety@springernature.com

Printed and bound by CPI Group (UK) Ltd, Croydon, CR0 4YY
30/09/2026
02225515-0007